Spirituality
Simplified

An Ideal Starting Point for Those New to the Spiritual Path

A Handy Reference Guide for Experienced Seekers

Jeff Maziarek

SpiritSimple Enterprises L.L.C.

Villa Park, Illinois

www.spiritsimple.com

Published by:

SpiritSimple Enterprises L.L.C.
P.O. Box 6973
Villa Park, IL 60181

First Edition: 2003

First Printing: Advance Special Issue printed in December 2002 as
Spirituality Made Simple by The Wordsmith's Anvil, 5114 Balcones
Woods Drive, #307, Austin, TX 78759 [www.wordsmithsanvil.com]

Author photograph by Andrea Maziarek
Cover art and graphics by Janet Jaffke (jjafke@comcast.net)
Page layout and pre-press services by Sally Elvart (innov8@inil.com)
Published by arrangement with the author.

Library of Congress Control Number: 2003096573

ISBN 0-9744841-0-5
Printed in the United States of America.

10 9 8 7 6 5 4 3

For reprint permissions or other information, address the Permissions
Department, SpiritSimple Enterprises L.L.C., P.O. Box 6973, Villa Park, IL,
60181.

Excerpts from the many written and lyrical works referenced in this book are
credited within the text of the chapters, and in the formal bibliography and
discography found in the Appendix.

#

This book offers the spiritual exploration of many aspects of life that may
include certain kinds of mental and emotional function and dysfunction. The
author in no way makes any diagnosis of any medical condition or prescribes any
medical or psychological treatment whatsoever. Any opinion, advice, technique,
or practice offered in this book is intended solely for spiritual purposes, and is
not to be construed to replace medical or other professional advice or treatment.

The author believes that if you need help, it is important to explore all that is
available to you for your well-being. If you suspect a medical or psychological
condition, consulting a qualified physician or therapist respectively is strongly
recommended.

Dedication

To the God-force, for giving me the privilege to be alive
on this unbelievably beautiful planet Earth

To my wonderful wife and best friend Andrea, for her unwavering
support, patience, and inspiration

To my late mother, Lorraine, for teaching me about compassion
and the importance of "staying in faith"

To my late father, Tony, for teaching me to write and to analyze,

To Codi and Heidi, for showing me every day what
unconditional love really means

Acknowledgments

Bringing *Spirituality Simplified* from concept to completion took more than four years, and candidly it would never have occurred without support and assistance from a number of people.

My most heartfelt gratitude goes out to:

Kaye O'Bara, for inspiring me to write in the first place

Andrea Maziarek, for being a constant source of love and support

Nancy Fleming-Walsch, for her interest in, and endorsement of this work

Brenda Ballard, a very talented editor, for enhancing the quality of my work

Noreen Damolaris, for her friendship, and for being such an incredible listener throughout my entire life

Peter & Elaine Cunningham, for facilitating my 4 month visit to the Greek island of Alonnisos

Rick Clark, for more than three decades of friendship, and for taking such excellent care of our dogs and home during our lengthy stays in Greece

Mary Lou Draper, for being such a loving friend, for providing top quality proofreading on the first draft manuscript, and for her unfailing support over the course of the entire project

Michele Martin, for greatly improving the grammar and flow of the first draft manuscript

Sue Spitler, for her insightful content-related editing input on parts of the first draft manuscript

Debby Steger, for top quality desktop publishing on the first draft manuscript, and for her support throughout the entire project

Janet Jaffke, for her beautiful book cover illustration and top-quality web-design services

Sally Elvart, for her exceptional page-layout and creative skills, and for coordinating production of the final manuscript

Mary and Pete Bosman, for content-related editing input on the final manuscript

Batavia, for selflessly sharing his experience with self-publishing

Gail Konz, for her ongoing spiritual advice and counsel

Renee White-Wagner, for her insightful guidance and for being such a wonderful friend; Renee you are such an angel!

Marty Weinstein, for his expert legal advice, and more importantly, for his unwavering loyalty and friendship

Dr. John Honey, for assisting me with physical healings, and for always reminding me of my Divine heritage

Jeanmarie Sullivan, for her amazing "presence" and creative networking, and for her zealous support of this work

Nicoletta Trenta, for always bringing a smile to my face during the 4 months I spent writing on Alonnisos

Bill Lewis and *John Pfeuffer,* for patronizing my technical writing business throughout the time this book was being written and beyond

Joseph Campbell, Deepak Chopra, Alan Cohen, Fr. Anthony DeMello, Wayne W. Dyer, Debbie Ford, Lynn Grabhorn, Louise Hay, Dan Millman, Arnold Patent, Eckhart Tolle, Neale Donald Walsch, Stuart Wilde, Marianne Williamson, and many other authors for following their inspiration to bring such valuable content to the world

Jackson Browne, Mike Campbell, John Corey, Dennis DeYoung, Dan Fogelberg, Don Henley, Will Jennings, John Lennon, Stan Lynch, Paul McCartney, Jack Nitzsche, Joe Puerta, Todd Rundgren, Buffy Sainte-Marie, J.D. Souther, Triumph, and Jai Winding for writing such marvelously inspiring and thought-provoking song lyrics.

I am also very grateful to the following individuals who were right there for me when I needed them at various times throughout this project:

Craig Astler, Joanne Berridge, Marla Bralles, Donna Corso, Bill DeMello, Susan Dabagia, Diandra, Mindy Franklin, Kris Griffith-O'Hara, Walt & Deb Griffith, Chris Hansen, Betty Hoeffner Linda Hooper, Mike Kapel, Jim Kinkaid, Lisa Jacobsen, Gary Madden, Keith Maziarek, Shirley McDaniel, Marie McMennamin, Jeanne Moriki, Rick Moser, Melissa Rabin, Kathy Stocker, Tom Strapp, the late Orville Warning and Linda Whitten

Table Of Contents

Introduction

Several years ago I heard someone on television say that there's a book in each of us just waiting to emerge. At that time I gave little, if any, credibility to that statement; it had never occurred to me that I would ever have anything of real value to share with the world. In fact, from the time I was in my late teens, my philosophy about creative pursuits such as art and writing was best summed up by this quote from a song by the 70's rock-n-roll band Ambrosia: "Art beware, it's all been done, there's nothing new under the sun."[1]

What finally inspired me to consider writing a book, however, was some very practical advice from a friend of mine: Kaye O'Bara. A truly wonderful woman, Kaye was the subject of *A Promise is A Promise*, a captivating book written by Dr. Wayne Dyer (Hay House: 1996) describing how she personally cared for her comatose daughter Edwarda for more than 26 years. In particular, during a visit to Kaye's Florida home in February of 1999, she strongly recommended that I write a book related to spirituality, for it was very evident to her that this was a subject for which I had great *passion*.

When I first sat down to write, I had little idea of what specifically it was that I should write about, nor did I have any insight into what type of work process to apply to a project of this nature. Nevertheless, I took Kaye's advice to heart, and began disciplining myself to squeeze book-writing time in between the writing projects I was doing as a freelance technical writer. "Writer's block" was indeed a constant companion in the early days of this creative effort, until one day it dawned on me that I simply needed to make a habit of asking the God-Force for guidance prior to sitting down to write

---

[1] Joe Puerta, Copyright © 1977 by Rubicon Music (BMI) (All rights reserved. Used by permission). From the album *Life Beyond L.A.*, (Warner Bros. Records, Inc. 1978).

on any given day. Once I adopted this approach, little-by-little the insights came, and ultimately *Spirituality Simplified* came into being.

The underlying passion that led to this work was the strong desire to create a spiritual growth book for mainstream readers that was both simple-to-understand, and that referenced literally the "best of the best" content from a broad assortment of personal/spiritual growth books that I'd read over nearly a decade. I believe that an introductory book about spirituality has long been needed; the sheer number of books available in these categories make it very challenging for any person interested in a path of self-discovery to choose which one to actually read *first!*

Spirituality Simplified is therefore intended primarily to serve as a starting point for anyone with a sincere desire to pursue a path of spiritual growth. Additionally, it is an ideal resource for any person already on this path, as it not only serves as a handy reference guide to basic spiritual principles, but also provides a virtual "roadmap" to the works of many of today's most respected spiritual teachers.

Specifically, within the pages of this book is guidance and example derived from what I have learned and experienced on this path, augmented by inspirational and/or thought-provoking passages on a number of topics from a host of authors, including such prominent names as: Deepak Chopra, Anthony DeMello, Dr. Wayne Dyer, Louise Hay, Don Miguel Ruiz, Eckhart Tolle, Neale Donald Walsch, Stuart Wilde, and many others.

Combined, this content is designed to first provide you with greater insight into the essential nature of both the God-Force and yourself, and secondly, to give you a solid overview of basic spiritual principles that is both easy-to-understand and entertaining.

Throughout this book you will also find recommendations for related reading, as well as several quotations from the lyrics of various pop music songs that directly relate to the particular subject being addressed. While the quotations would obviously have greater impact if you were actually listening to the songs, my purpose in using them in this format is to demonstrate that a great deal of modern music does indeed include meaningful messages. The bottom line is that music isn't merely capable of "calming the savage beast," but can also be a valuable spiritual growth resource if you pay closer attention to the words of the songs that you hear.

In closing this welcome to *Spirituality Simplified*, I want you to know that I greatly appreciate your interest in this work, and sincerely hope that you derive as much value from reading it as I did from researching and writing it.

If after reading *Spirituality Simplified* you have any comments or questions regarding it, please feel free to contact me by referring to the Author Contact page located at the back of the book.

1: Open-mindedness

There's a heaven on earth,
that so few ever find,
But the map's in your soul,
and the road's in your mind. [2]

DAN FOGELBERG
"THE WILD PLACES"

In order to move beyond the world we've always known and explore the myriad possibilities that are always available, it's absolutely critical that we learn to approach new information with an open mind. While this certainly isn't a revolutionary new insight, the plain and simple fact is that most people have a difficult time when it comes to being genuinely open-minded.

The underlying reason it is often challenging to accept new concepts is that an individual's belief system effectively serves as the foundation for how he or she processes the world. Core beliefs are usually developed early in life, and, as such, are typically deeply rooted within the person's consciousness. When an individual encounters new information that challenges a belief that is near and dear to him or her, the initial reaction is often one of defensiveness. Moreover, if one is emotionally attached to the particular belief, then the reaction will be even more intense. We can usually see this manifested most clearly when beliefs about *religion* or *spirituality* are questioned in any way.

According to F. Scott Fitzgerald, "The test of a first-rate intelligence is the ability to hold two opposed ideas in the mind at the same time, and still retain the ability to function." [3] This observation is directly related to the process of developing open-mindedness, for as we take in new information, our existing beliefs and judgments naturally

---

[2] Daniel Fogelberg, Copyright © 1990 by EMI April Music Inc./Hickory Grove Music (ASCAP) (All rights reserved. Used by permission.) From the CD *Wild Places*, (CBS Records and manufactured by Epic Records. 1990).

[3] Francis Scott Key Fitzgerald, 1896-1940

remain rooted in our minds. We need to be willing to at least consider new information that doesn't fit our established beliefs, without immediately judging it to be incorrect, or simply tuning it out.

Contrary to popular opinion – on the path of spiritual growth – being open-minded does not mean being gullible. It represents being truly accepting of the fact that in the realm of spirituality 'anything is possible'. For example, if someone were to tell you that they woke in the middle of the night and actually saw an apparition of a dead relative, what would your initial reaction be? My guess is, that for most people, it would be one of skepticism. Yet, can you without a shadow of a doubt, prove that this individual did not actually see the deceased person they describe to you? The answer is *no*, of course you can't, and in turn, neither can they prove to you that they actually did see that person.

OPEN-MINDEDNESS AND RELIGION

Maintaining an open mind in the face of information that challenges accepted religious beliefs is especially difficult for most people. The reason is often obvious: religion usually provides the cornerstone upon which people build their entire life philosophy. While other aspects of life may be in chaos, religious principles can reliably ensure that a person's spiritual life remains essentially stable and predictable.

As the old saying goes, 'if you want to avoid conflict, don't discuss religion and politics'. Yet, if you do not even consider alternative religious viewpoints, then how do you succeed in developing a well-rounded view of life? In reality, many people shy away from even considering other religious points of view, because doing so would only serve to complicate their lives.

Primary Value of Religion

One of the most important things religion does is to make life easier by providing people with a set of rules (e.g., commandments), and other doctrines or dogma that establish the core philosophy to which the person is expected to adhere.

According to the author Stuart Wilde, religious philosophy in effect serves as "glue to hold the group together in a psychic bonding. In fact, the word *religion* comes from the Latin word *religare*, which means to bind."[4]

Once a person becomes 'bound' to the core philosophy, then no real thought or contemplation of existence is necessary, simply because that philosophy effectively removes the need to consider these higher aspects of life. This way of living is very appealing, because the act of questioning the so-called 'truth' requires an individual to expend quite a bit of energy to escape the psychic bonds of their particular religious group. Moreover, it demands that a person be willing to wander off philosophically and 'step into the unknown'.

Let's face it; it is far easier to stay within the status quo than to move outside it and strike out into uncharted territory. Nevertheless, staying with what feels safe and comfortable essentially does nothing to assist anyone in coming to an understanding of his or her higher purpose in life.

At the deepest level, there probably isn't a person alive today that does not in some way long to have some insight into the real meaning of their life. However, to gain any insight at all requires that a person be willing to step outside of the *alleged* safety of the 'known'.

This takes courage, and requires open-mindedness as well, because it often leads to situations in which one is exposed to new concepts that may be contrary to their traditional religious or spiritual philosophy.

OPEN-MINDEDNESS AND 'ECCENTRIC' RELIGIOUS/SPIRITUAL PRACTICES

Naturally, it becomes quite a bit more challenging to remain open-minded when you encounter religious and/or spiritual practices that are viewed by the mainstream as eccentric, or even outlandish in nature.

---

[4] Stuart Wilde, *The Quickening*, (Carlsbad, CA: Hay House, Inc., 1996), p. 91

For example, it really is quite difficult for the average person (including this writer) to look at a group of cult members that commits mass suicide in order to get a ride on a passing spaceship heading to heaven, and say "anything is possible." In such circumstances, I recommend that you learn to evaluate what you judge to be eccentric beliefs or spiritual practices, as processes which an individual needs to go through in the course of coming to know who they are at the deepest level.

As mentioned previously, we human beings have so little knowledge of the inner workings of the Universe that we are not in a position of authority to question another person's religious or spiritual beliefs. In general, do your best to adopt the following perspective: as long as it's not hurting other individuals in any way, then whatever spiritual practices a person undertakes is his or her choice and responsibility.

DEVELOPING OPEN-MINDEDNESS

Developing an open-minded approach to life is not an easy thing for many people, and even more difficult for people who hold to very rigid belief systems. As with anything in life, however, becoming more open-minded simply requires regular practice on your part.

One way to develop open-mindedness is to begin *observing yourself* as you are being exposed to new concepts or ideas. To do this, you essentially take the role of a witness to the process, as well as being an active participant in it. While it may sound challenging, it really is not. All that is required is for you to actively pay attention to what you are reading and hearing, and then acknowledge your judgments one-by-one as they crop up.

If you are uncertain what "witnessing yourself" means, think back to a time in your life when you may have said something to yourself like, "my mind is playing tricks on me." If you live under the common premise that your mind is who you are, then ponder this for a moment: *Who is it that made that statement?* Did the mind make that statement about itself, or is there some other entity that stands outside of the mind at all times?

The answer is that your mind or brain may be the command center of the body, but the *commander* is actually an awareness you have of yourself, which is situated outside of the brain or mind. Looking at it another way, consider the mind as the 'me' you speak of when you refer to yourself, and the 'I' as that higher part of you that essentially observes the 'me' as your life evolves. We'll discuss this concept of the 'me' and the 'I' in full detail in Chapter 3: *Who Are You?*

As you learn to 'witness yourself', you develop the ability to immediately recognize when you are judging, and *in that moment* remind yourself to remain open-minded. It is important to note, however, that witnessing gets much more difficult when new information challenges a belief to which you are very attached. In these instances, your belief system typically responds with an emotionally-charged judgment, requiring you to exhibit even greater determination toward maintaining the role of an independent observer.

As you begin working on developing your witnessing skills, do your best to remain patient with yourself when you find it challenging to remain open-minded, and always remember the old adage that "practice makes perfect."

HOW I BECAME MORE OPEN-MINDED

Having been raised as a Roman Catholic, I fully understand just how powerful the bonds to group philosophy can become. Throughout my childhood and well into my teens, I did not question the dogma of the church, either at home or in Catholic schools. It simply never occurred to me to challenge any of the rules, or any biblical accounts.

When I reached my mid-thirties, however, I experienced a business failure that ultimately led to a radical change in my perspective on life. In particular, as a result of this significant career setback, I was serendipitously introduced to a very insightful individual; a person who helped me open my mind to concepts I would never have even considered in the past. The individual of whom I write had proven psychic skills, along with the ability to communicate directly with the spiritual world.

It's quite possible that, if you are like most people, the previous sentence invited some amount of doubt to creep into your mind. That is not surprising, when one considers that the world of the paranormal is typically not given much credibility in the mainstream world, especially with all of the questionable 1-900 psychic lines on television these days. Like most people, I too had my doubts about the entire concept of clairvoyance, but after I invested in my first 'reading' with this person back in 1992, those doubts quickly disappeared.

When we sat down to get started, I must admit my skepticism continued; however, within minutes that changed as I was told several details about my life that could not possibly have been learned prior to our meeting. These were not general statements, and this individual also didn't throw out 'trial balloon' comments waiting for me to add more content that could then be built upon. What I had found was a total stranger offering me information about my life experiences that was incredibly detailed, and unbelievably accurate.

As the reading closed and we began a normal conversation, we glided into a discussion about the practice of spirit channeling and its relationship to spirituality. It was then that spiritual philosophy was shared with me that was much different than anything I had been exposed to in the past. This psychically-gifted person spoke of many things that day, including Spirit Guides, Angels, the Higher Self/Soul, the afterlife, and much more. I was also left with the admonition that I needed to work harder at developing the spiritual side of my life.

This person and I would have many other conversations over a period of four years, and during that time was one of several people who played an important role in opening my mind to new possibilities. However, I was never really told to believe anything in particular, other than that I was a blessed child of God, a 'spark of the

Divine', who was deeply loved by his creator. Neither was there any attempt to convert me to any type of religion or organized spiritual practice, other than perhaps some form of daily meditation.

If I had not first seen this individual demonstrate her skills so convincingly, I wouldn't have been as inclined to consider the information she shared with me about spirituality. Essentially, because she was able to establish a level of credibility with me early on in our relationship, it was easier for me to 'let down my guard', and eventually become significantly more open-minded than I had ever been in the past.

Anything Is Possible

In the end, the primary lesson I learned – when it came to spirituality – was that indeed, *anything is possible*, and since we cannot clearly see the 'big picture', it's inappropriate to judge another person's spiritual practices.

From what I have discovered so far, we simply cannot know for certain what is 'true' and what is 'not true', because absolute truth is an elusive commodity. There is no single right way, there are in fact *many* ways. Each of us has such a limited perspective on the cosmos that we simply cannot say without reservation that something is absolutely right or absolutely wrong.

For those who think that science can thoroughly prove something to be right or wrong, think again! For its entire prowess, the scientific community remains unable to tell us what makes the heart of a fetus *begin* beating. For those who feel that traditional religious dogma defines what is right and wrong, remember that what one religion claims to be the "Word of God" does not always align with what another says.

In all instances, what religious ideology claims as truth has been handed down over generations from one person to another, with each new storyteller or writer likely adding their own bit of journalistic license to the mix. In the end, what we are told is the "Word of God" is something that we had to have been introduced to by someone else, and based on that introduction, we are expected to blindly accept it because that is what a good Christian, or Muslim, or Hindu, etc. should do. Yet, haven't you ever wondered how the God-Force could apply different rules to different groups of people?

To dare question the source of the information provided in religious texts is often considered by many religions to be at least inappropriate, and at worst sinful. The reality is that individual religious dogma cannot prove its own truth is actually *the* truth, nor can it prove that another religion's truth is not *the truth*. Once you open your mind to this fact, it becomes easier and easier to be more open-minded about spirituality in general.

Open-mindedness & Spiritual Growth

Based on the information contained in this chapter, it is not hard to conclude that spiritual growth requires that we develop a more open-minded attitude toward alternative spiritual concepts, philosophies and practices.

If you are inclined to work at becoming more open-minded, and are at a stage in your life where you are willing to consider new possibilities with respect to your own spiritual path, read on!

2: Who or What is God?

You never have to get down your knees,
You don't have to holler, 'please, please
No, you never have to get down on your knees
For a little tin God.[5]

DON HENLEY
"LITTLE TIN GOD"

'Who am I to address this question?' was a naturally occurring thought as I began to write this chapter. Let's face it: the truth is the only time any of us will absolutely know for certain who or what God really is, is when we finally leave this planet, moving on to the next dimension. For centuries mystics have reported that the reality of God is truly unknowable. Nonetheless, throughout recorded history men and women have shared their opinions and viewpoints about the essence of God, the Creator, the All-That-Is, and so on.

Why – since the dawning of human life – have people continually theorized about God's nature? Simply put, deep within each of us there is a strong yearning to know where we come from, and to where we will ultimately go whenever we do leave this treasured planet.

While that longing exists in all people, many tend to block it out because it is too complex to think about when more pressing day-to-day concerns surround them. Others ignore the longing because they don't know quite how to reflect or where to look for the answers. Coming to an understanding of the true nature of God often takes a backseat to earning the day-to-day living and dealing with the challenges associated with human relationships. Because of these obstacles, many people in the so-called 'civilized world' have chosen to look to traditional religion for answers.

---

[5] Don Henley, Danny Kortchmar and J.D. Souther © Copyright 1989 Cass County Music/Kortchmar Music/Ice Age Music (ASCAP) (All rights reserved. Used by permission.) From the CD *The End of the Innocence*, (The David Geffen Company, manufactured exclusively by Warner Bros. Records, Inc., a Time Warner Company. 1988).

THE TRADITIONAL VIEW OF GOD

In a typical Western religion, God is usually depicted as a "white-bearded male who roams around the sky creating the world."[6] This God is a Being that controls all things occurring in the Universe, knows exactly what everyone does, and is aware when His laws or commandments are being broken. The idea of punishment for one's sins is at the foundation of this view of God; this God/Father holds us accountable for our wrongdoing. The errors we make are then "judged by various interpreters of his laws who throughout history have claimed access to the Divine."[7]

Over the centuries, a great many people have accepted the words of these privileged interpreters (e.g., priests, ministers, rabbis, religious scholars) as absolute truth; to doubt — in any way — the validity of their interpretations would be considered a sin. It is interesting that most people are unwilling to either question the authority of these individuals, or to be skeptical concerning the religious texts that allegedly contain the "Word of God." Why?

Recall that it is often far simpler to accept this information as 'truth' than to take the time and energy to question it. Organized religions often effectively wrap everything up in a nice package, requiring little, if any, serious contemplation by followers regarding the nature of existence.

Stuart Wilde in *The Quickening,* illustrates the general willingness to blindly accept religious dogma as absolute truth.

> *If you knew nothing about Christianity and you*
> *had never heard of the Bible, you would pick up the*
> *book and ask the critical question, 'Who wrote*
> *this stuff?' Err…well, actually no one knows.*
> *But, it's the sacred channeled word of God.*[8]

---

[6] Wayne W. Dyer, *Manifest Your Destiny*, (New York: HarperCollins, 1997) p. 21

[7] Ibid., p. 21

[8] Stuart Wilde, *The Quickening*, op. cit., p. 94

The very questioning of the origin of the Bible is often considered sacrilegious by many a devout Christian, but is it unreasonable to want to know who wrote such an important literary work? Of course not.

It is not solid reasoning, in my view, to simply accept the entire Bible as the "Word of God," solely because a religion or religions *say* that it is. Why not? Because it has a number of inconsistencies and contradictions. For example, the Old Testament contains a fair share of violence with turmoil, and includes memorable passages such as the oft-quoted "an eye for an eye," while the teachings of Jesus in the New Testament include admonitions such as "love ye one another" and "turn the other cheek." Which of these clearly conflicting messages, then, is the actual Word of God? Or, are we to assume that God has different rules for different periods of time?

Within the New Testament itself there are discrepancies, most notably four separate Gospels that each tell a different version of the same story. If the Gospels in the New Testament are actually the sacred inspired words of God, then why are they not more consistent in their content? Once again, according to Stuart Wilde:

> *One would have to presume that either God had an incredibly poor memory, or he had some kind of cosmic twitch whereby every decade or so he would sit bolt upright and, for no explainable reason, blurt out the story he told years back, forgetting what he said the last time.* [9]

While Mr. Wilde's comment certainly has a tongue-in-cheek flavor, his observation is nonetheless thought-provoking. One possible explanation is that the four Gospels were not literally the inspired words of God, but instead a collection of stories written and then passed on from generation to generation. This could explain the

---

[9] Ibid., p. 97

inconsistency of the content – as should be fairly obvious to anyone – that stories which are handed down tend to change over time, as each storyteller adds his or her own interpretation and personal flavor to the material.

The Value in Religious Texts

So, does the preceding commentary imply that there is nothing of value in the Bible, or in any other of the major religious texts for that matter? By no means; there is no doubt that religious texts contain meaningful and helpful information; the key is to discern which of it is of value to you as you move along *your* path of self-discovery.

I have personally found some aspects of the Psalms in the Old Testament (e.g., the 23rd and 91st Psalms) to be of value in my spiritual growth, as well as some excerpts from the Book of Job. For example, one of the most powerful quotations within the Book of Job, is when Job says, "the thing I feared has come upon me," (Job 3:25); a statement which I believe refers to the power of our thoughts to attract to us whatever we focus upon — *whether we consciously want it or not.*

That quote helped make me more mindful of how important it is to remain aware of what I am concentrating my thought and feeling energies upon, so as to not let fear or negativity dominate my consciousness. From this passage, I also came to the critical realization that worrying was a total waste of energy, and therefore extremely counterproductive.

This is just one example of the valuable information that is available in the Holy Bible, and without question, other prominent religious texts (e.g., the Koran, the Kabbalah, and so on) provide worthy content as well. Basically, the important thing is to approach these texts with a discerning attitude that leads you to accept only that information which makes sense to you, and which, in your heart, *feels* right to you.

Traditional Religious Concepts and Fear

While traditional religions are capable of providing a stable foundation for spiritual growth, those that represent God as a monarch who punishes his or her subjects for their transgressions are not by any means empowering their followers.

To the contrary, by rigidly adhering to such traditional religious beliefs, one is often motivated more out of fear than loyalty or love. For example, "I'd better follow God's commandments (rules) or I'll be disliked by the other members of my church, or worse yet, be punished in hell for my sins."

This fear works to get people mechanically altering their behavior at times, but it does not provide for true long-term shifts in a person's beliefs and consciousness. In my experience, people simply aren't inspired to delve into new ways of thinking and behaving when the motivation to do so is based on the threat of punishment. Profound changes usually happen when people see some form of tangible reward for undertaking the effort necessary to make those changes.

In many instances the fear-based motivation characterizing some traditional religious doctrines, can exercise control over an individual for an entire lifetime. For most, it is simply too intimidating to go against the immediate family, the tribe, or the church. So, they choose to accept the status quo and not deal with the conflict that would result from questioning that specific doctrine. While this approach is certainly much easier, ultimately it limits an individual's spiritual growth potential, because it truly inhibits them from coming to a better understanding of 'who they really are'.

Adherence to traditional religious doctrines is clearly the norm in many cultures around the world, but throughout history there have been a number of alternative views of God, as well as a wide range of religious practices. It is not my intent, however, to provide an exhaustive discussion of the myriad ways that God has been defined and worshipped throughout recorded history; there are perhaps thousands of theology books available which address this subject.

Rather, my purpose in this work is simply to share with you the view that I've adopted regarding God-Force: one that is not in any way based on traditional religious doctrine.

AN ALTERNATIVE VIEW OF GOD

What if the God-Force isn't the judging, punishing Creator that is described in the Old Testament of the Bible and referred to similarly in other religious texts as well? What if, instead, God is actually "universal intelligence flowing through everything, inspiring the natural process to unfold"?[10]

In this view, God is not a monarch that manages and controls all natural events that occur on planet Earth. Rather, God is a pure, loving energy that is constantly creating in form *through us*, for He cannot actually *experience* creation in form (i.e., the third dimension) without us.

This view of God is strongly expressed in the NY Times bestseller *Conversations with God, Book 1* by Neale Donald Walsch. In this first installment of the critically acclaimed three-book series, Mr. Walsch claims that God directly made this statement to him regarding His/Her/Its true nature:

> *If you believe that God is some omnipotent being who*
> *hears all prayers, says "yes" to some, "no" to others,*
> *and "maybe, but not now" to the rest, you are mistaken.*
> *By what rule of thumb would God decide?*
> *If you believe that God is the creator*
> *and decider of all things in your life, you are mistaken.*
> *God is the observer, not the creator.*[11]

This is clearly nowhere close to the description of God that is provided by most traditional religions, and yet from all that I have read

---

[10] Wayne W. Dyer, *Manifest Your Destiny*, op. cit., p. 22
[11] Neale Donald Walsch, *Conversations with God, Book 1* (New York: G.P. Putnam's Sons, 1996) p. 13

and learned on the path of self-discovery, it makes great sense. Why would God give us free will and then punish us for doing something against a set of commandments? This passage from Walsch's *Conversations with God, Book 3*, builds upon this point:

> *There is no free will if to exercise it in certain*
> *ways produces punishment. That makes a mockery*
> *of free will and renders it counterfeit.*[12]

A Judgmental God?

Why, then, do so many people simply accept the idea of a judgmental God? There are probably dozens of reasons, but in the end it ultimately comes down to the fact that *someone told them to* adopt this view of God. The reality is until we each begin the quest to discover our own personal truths, we are all just a collection of beliefs that were handed down to us by those whose beliefs were, in essentially all instances, handed down to them as well.

To paraphrase the late Fr. Tony DeMello, most of our core beliefs are typically not our own anyway; they actually belong to Mom or Dad, Grandma or Grandpa, or some other adult that had a major impact on us when we were children. This is not to suggest that beliefs cannot change over time, because they surely can, but it does imply that it is very difficult to identify a core belief that comes from any original thought of our own.

The Belief-Review Process

As mentioned previously in Chapter 1, beliefs form the foundation for a person's life, so changing any fundamental belief in particular can be very challenging, and even more so if your family's opinion remains a dominant influence in your life. However, once you make the decision to become more open-minded, it actually is increasingly

---

[12] Neale Donald Walsch, Conversations with God, Book 3, (Charlottesville, VA: Hampton Roads Publishing Company, Inc., 1998) p. 253

easy to look at all of your beliefs in a more detached way.

This 'belief-review' process takes a bit of effort, but the potential rewards are significant as you come to the realization that perhaps much of what you've accepted as the truth actually serves to limit your possibilities for meaningful spiritual growth. As my own awareness began to grow, I initially found myself particularly protective of my longstanding beliefs, because, again, it is always much simpler to just remain the same than it is to allow change into our lives. Over the past ten years, however, I have personally evolved to the point where it's fairly simple for me to question any of my longstanding beliefs, and for the most part to always be open to new information.

Simply put, it just takes some practice at being the 'witness' that looks upon your life from the perspective of an observer. Once you develop some proficiency at being the detached observer of your life, you will find yourself being less emotionally attached to your beliefs. In my own life, there are times these days when I'll look back at some of the old beliefs that were important to me, and I am actually amazed that I could have ever believed so many things that were not the least bit sustaining for me.

To me, the whole idea that God is some monarch in the sky who is keeping tabs on all of our choices is not reasonable. From a purely logical perspective, it doesn't make sense that the Creator, the All That Is, the Pure Love of the Cosmos who loves *without condition*, actually 'makes a list and checks it twice to find out who's naughty and nice.' It really is somewhat amusing to think that the Creator who gave us 'free will choice' now sits back and keeps moment-to-moment score of how each of us are doing with respect to obeying His/Her/Its commandments. Preposterous in my view, but an incredible number of people throughout the world believe it, making it exceptionally easy for many traditional religions to manipulate their behavior through the application of fear-based motivation (e.g., threats of Divine punishment) and guilt.

God as Co-Creator

From all that I've read and *experienced*, I have come to believe that the God-Force is not some autocratic monarch in the sky, but is actually a purely loving energy that supports us in our growth in a detached manner. We are therefore not the subjects of some 'Cosmic King' with no power of our own, but are instead individual pieces of God-consciousness with the ability to *co-create* with God that which we desire. If you doubt this to be true, then consider these words from Jesus about his own miracle making, "He who believes in me, the works that I do he also shall do; and greater than these he shall do."[13]

Now clearly this concept of co-creation carries with it enormous responsibility, for it means that in the end it is you who are fully responsible for everything that you experience in your life. However, it is also incredibly empowering; as long as you maintain the notion that something or someone else is out there doing things *to* you, you effectively render yourself powerless to do anything about it.

WHICH VIEW OF GOD WORKS FOR YOU?

When one compares this alternate view of God against the traditional view of God, it is strikingly obvious that the two views are diametrically opposed. So, which of these views of God works for you? If you're reading this book, it's likely that the traditional view isn't working for you anymore, or perhaps it never really did in the first place.

Your Philosophical Challenge

At this point, you may be facing the challenge of transitioning to a new spiritual philosophy, while your family and friends maintain their connections to the old. This can be very difficult to handle, particularly if one's parents, relatives, and friends are devoutly

---

[13] John 14:12

committed to traditional religious practice.

Your decision to step away from tradition may expose you to significant criticism, as well as pressure to return to the fold. This passage from Stuart Wilde's *The Quickening* advances this very point:

> *You can imagine how hard it is for a person*
> *who is raised a Catholic to walk away from his church*
> *and to live with the thought that, if the church is right,*
> *when he gets to the Pearly Gates, Jesus will be*
> *there wagging his finger and that individual will*
> *be cast into hell for that eternity. That's heavy.*
> *You need a lot of individuality, strength, and*
> *personal charisma to walk away*
> *from a manipulation that intense.*[14]

I can personally relate to this passage as – much to the chagrin of my parents, particularly my mother – I made the decision to leave Catholicism behind in the early 1990s. Although both my mother and father were disappointed in me, and did make some effort to convince me to reconsider my position, fortunately I was spared any significant coercion to return to the flock. The same cannot be said for others I have encountered that have left their churches, as it was not uncommon for the *tribe* to place enormous pressure on these individuals to 'come to their senses'. That is unfortunate, but clearly not surprising given how seriously many people take both their religion and church affiliations.

BREAKING FREE OF RELIGIOUS TRADITION

If you find yourself wanting to branch out and develop your own spiritual philosophy, but are concerned about any repercussions that may result, remember that ultimately being true to yourself (i.e., seeking self-approval) is far more important than living for the

---

[14] Stuart Wilde, *The Quickening*, op. cit., p. 93

approval of others. While this may sound like clichéd advice, consider this: throughout your life, has receiving the approval of others ever really provided you with any real peace-of-mind or long-lasting contentment?

I'll take the liberty of answering for you: *no*, it hasn't. Do you know why not? Approval is fleeting, as it can quickly change to condemnation the moment you do something that someone judges to be inappropriate or wrong. So instead of being focused on pleasing others, have the courage to change your focus toward pleasing yourself, and you will ultimately discover a great truth– seeking approval from outside yourself is a total waste of time.

Once you do decide to strike out on your own, it's my experience that any pressure you'll encounter will naturally be the fiercest at the start. If you can endure the initial criticism and manipulative efforts without giving in, what you will find in most cases is that your family and friends will eventually back off, and the balance of the religious tribe will ultimately give up on you, directing their attention towards another 'lost sheep' that has strayed from the fold. At that point, what you'll discover is that you will begin attracting new people in your life to replace those old religion/church-based connections, and these individuals will most likely be on a similar path of spiritual discovery.

Within a very short time of discovering the so-called 'spiritual path', I found myself meeting and interacting with a wide variety of new people. The conversations with these individuals were typically invigorating and uplifting, as the excitement of sharing new ideas led to very energetic exchanges of information. While I was not always completely comfortable with some of the views and/or practices I learned about, the admonition I'd previously been given to remain open-minded helped me make my best efforts to listen with a minimum of judgment, and to continue remembering that in the realm of spirituality truly anything is possible.

As you move forward in developing your own personal spiritual philosophy/God-view, one suggestion I'd make is that you not limit yourself with respect to what books you will read, tapes to which you will listen, or concepts you will consider. From my experience, it is wise to collect as much information as possible, and follow your gut instincts regarding what *feels* right for you as you create your own personal spiritual philosophy. As you proceed on this journey of spiritual self-discovery, you might also consider keeping a journal of the thoughts and feelings you experience as you reflect upon the various ideas you encounter.

The Path of Spiritual Growth & Organized Religious Practice

It is important to emphasize here that embarking on this path does not necessarily preclude you from remaining involved in some form of organized religious practice. You can indeed be a spiritual seeker and still participate in conventional church activities. However, from what I've seen, within a relatively short time you may find yourself feeling a bit estranged from the old ways, particularly if you have made progress in developing your open-mindedness.

As you grow spiritually, you may feel increasingly challenged to remain connected to your past religious affiliations, largely because *your* awareness is increasing while the rest of the congregation has essentially remained the same. People will sense something different about you from an energy perspective, because as your awareness grows you will actually emit a different "vibe" than you did in the past. You may ultimately find that you have quite simply outgrown the old practice and as a result, feel the desire to leave it behind completely. On the other hand, you might just become even more comfortable in your established religious practice as a result of your broadened perspective.

In either case, my advice is to follow your heart, and trust that in the end all will work out for your highest good and that of all concerned.

COMMUNICATING TO GOD THROUGH PRAYER

Any discussion about the nature of God[15] would be incomplete without some mention of the concept of prayer, for it serves as part of the foundation for virtually all-spiritual and/or religious practice. My purpose here is not to provide a comprehensive discourse about prayer – as there already exist hundreds, if not thousands, of books related to this subject. Instead, I will just touch upon it, my primary objective being to share information with you regarding the use of prayer as a very practical spiritual tool.

If you speak to individuals with a spiritual and/or religious orientation, it is likely you will find that a majority of them pray on a regular basis, with many doing so more than once per day. Moreover, even those people who do not consider themselves religious or spiritual will often be quick to pray when they encounter a particularly challenging life situation.

Prayer tends to be, in effect, an automatic action whenever true danger is present. Witness those who survive major plane crashes typically reporting hearing the name of God being screamed throughout the cabin at the moment of impact.

The practice of prayer is generally taught early in life, and the methods used to pray, as well as prayers themselves vary in countless ways. In my case, while growing up Catholic, I was fed a steady diet of 'Our Fathers' and 'Hail Marys', which I normally said in a rote fashion without any real understanding about either what I was saying, or why I was saying it.

After about two-and-a-half decades of that type of prayer, I stopped praying for a few years, to begin again soon after I started my journey down the path of spiritual growth back in 1992. In particular, during that time I was introduced to various Bible psalms, as well as other biblical content, and was also exposed to the power of

---

[15] All references to either God or the God-Force are interchangeable for the purposes of this work.

affirmations, which are, in effect, another form of prayer.

While a certain segment of the U.S. population will likely equate affirmations with the satirical TV character Stuart Smalley on reruns of Saturday Night Live, (i.e., "I'm good enough, I'm smart enough, and doggone-it, people like me."), my experience has demonstrated that they can be an incredibly valuable personal growth tool. If you can come to an understanding of the basic principles underlying them, say them frequently, (and also remember to write them as present-tense statements of fact), you can indeed manifest any number of things in your life.

The Value of Affirmations and Prayer

For example, through the regular use of affirmations added to another manifestation technique (*see Chapter 10*), over a period of nine years I was regularly able to attract new customers for my technical writing services. During this time frame, virtually nothing was invested in marketing my services, yet each time I was in need of new work assignments, the phone *always* rang with the exact amount of work that I desired (neither more nor less). Interestingly, during those occasional times when I lost faith in affirmations and other spiritual practices, and felt compelled to go 'make something happen' by consciously pursuing new business opportunities, the phone *never* rang in response to those forced marketing efforts.

Although affirmations played (and continue to play) an important role in my daily spiritual practice, prayer remains a key element of it as well. For years I used a variety of prayers, many of which were characteristically traditional in nature; I still continue to use some of these prayers because I find them very comforting and empowering to say. However, my overall prayer practice changed dramatically back in 1997 when I discovered this quotation in *Conversations with God, Book 1*:

> *You will not have that for which you ask,*
> *nor can you have anything you want. This is because*

*your very request is a statement of lack, and your
saying you want a thing only works to produce
that precise experience—wanting—in your reality.
The correct prayer is therefore never a prayer
of supplication, but a prayer of gratitude.*[16]

Now, read this passage again slowly and let it sink in for a bit…

Did the thought cross your mind that being grateful for what has
yet to manifest itself in your life appears to be somewhat backward?
It really is quite reasonable, however, when you stop to realize that
the Scriptures of essentially all major religions are very clear about
the creative power of human thought. For example, remember the
oft-quoted Bible verse that says, *"For as a man thinketh in his heart,
so is he."*[17]

If you take this statement literally, the statement is promising you
that when you really *want* something, your thoughts (and feelings)
are actually focused on the *wanting* and not the *having*. The only
result, therefore, can be that you stay in a wanting state, which in
effect serves to keep away that which you wish to experience. On
the contrary, if you adopt the practice of being grateful in advance of
having a particular desire fulfilled, you are essentially affirming the
inevitability of its fulfillment.

Personally speaking, the words contained in the preceding quotation were, without question, life-changing, for they shook the very
foundation of my views about how to pray. From the moment I
read those words, I stopped approaching God for anything, but
instead adopted the practice of simply thanking God in advance for
that which I desire to experience. This doesn't mean that I expect
God to simply 'deliver the goods', because as we learned earlier in
this chapter, it is not God's function to create or un-create the

---

[16] Neale Donald Walsch, *Conversations with God, Book 1*, op. cit., p. 11
[17] Proverbs 23:7

circumstances of our lives.

Rather, this approach to prayer is about having enough confidence
in my co-creative power with God to know that the satisfaction of
any sincere desire is essentially a foregone conclusion. Using it has
produced excellent results for me; I have found that things now
come more easily to me than at any other time in my life.

FAITH IS THE KEY

Not surprisingly, for this method of prayer to produce the results
you desire it is absolutely critical that you have *faith*. But what
exactly is faith? According to St. Paul, "Faith is the substance of
things hoped for, the evidence of things not seen."[18] In the words of
Dr. Joseph Murphy:

> *Faith is a fusion of your thought and feeling,*
> *or your mind and heart, which is so complete,*
> *inflexible, and impregnable that no external*
> *events or happenings can move you.*[19]

To me, faith means that you have such confidence in the certainty
of something occurring, that you truly have not one ounce of doubt
about it. Or, as I once heard Dr. Wayne Dyer say during a live presentation, "faith is not a *belief* that you will have that which you
desire, but rather a confident, inner *knowing* that you will." The
difference is simple: A belief is a theoretical concept, one that can be
easily affected by doubt. Knowing, on the other hand, is something
that comes from direct experience of your own life, and thus exists
within you, unencumbered by doubt.

For example, you could have a belief that you can swim, but you
will only know that it is possible when you actually get into a pool

---

[18] Hebrews 11:1

[19] Dr. Joseph Murphy, *The Amazing Laws of Cosmic Mind Power*, (W. Nyack, NY:
Parker Publishing Company, Inc. 1965) p. 29

or the ocean and experience it. Once you have this under your belt, from that point on you will absolutely *know* from direct physical experience that you can swim, and you will maintain this confidence for the rest of your life.

This same principle applies to everything you want to manifest in your life, as you need to have a *knowing* – not simply a belief – that what you desire will come to pass. But is it really possible to have an undying faith that your most heartfelt desires will be fulfilled? In a word, *YES!* If you doubt this is true, ask yourself the following questions: Do you *believe* that the most recent meal you consumed will be automatically and efficiently digested, or do you *know* it? Do you *believe* that your heart will instantly adjust its beat rate to accommodate for increased physical activity, or do you *know* it?

The answers are obvious, of course; you absolutely *know* that all critical life processes will be taken care of automatically, so you never give them a second thought. Why then is it that the majority of human beings are unable to apply that same mentality to the other elements of their lives? Namely, why is it that we can trust the God-Force to literally keep our bodies alive, but we do not feel comfortable trusting that higher aspect of ourselves to assist us in bringing the right people and/or circumstances into our lives at precisely the right time? And, why can't we have confidence that our material needs and desires will be fulfilled just as easily as our physiological needs are?

Learned Fear Opposes Faith

There is one very basic answer to these and all similar questions: at some point we were each taught at some level to be *afraid*, and our fear then transformed into a lack of trust in the God-Force for anything other than life itself.

This undercurrent of fear has plagued mankind for generation upon generation, despite the assurances of God's love that are found in virtually all religious texts.

Consider for example, this passage from the Gospel of Matthew:

Look at the birds of the air: they neither
sow nor reap nor gather into barns, and yet
your heavenly father feeds them. Are you not
of more value than they?[20]

As more sentient beings, we are at the very least of *comparable* value as the birds of the air or the flowers of the field. Nonetheless, we still have our nagging doubts that our needs will actually be met by simply remaining in faith, and staying focused on what we desire to create in our lives.

DEVELOPING TRUST IN GOD

So how *do* we overcome our fear and doubts and truly begin to trust in the God-force? From personal experience, the only way to learn to "let go and let God" is to *practice* doing so, moment-by-moment, one day at a time. You simply start by turning smaller problems or issues over to the God-Force (i.e., the Higher part of you) at the moment you encounter them.

For example, when you are about to meet with a person with whom you have historically had difficulties, try saying the following statement to yourself, *"I call upon the God-Force to speak through me in this interaction, and I am grateful for the opportunity to see this individual anew, as the Divine creation they truly are."* If you say this statement with sincere feeling, you will notice that the nature of the interaction will be much improved, simply because you put your 'little self' aside and allowed your 'Higher Self' to come to the forefront.

You can apply this same approach to every challenging or annoying situation that you encounter (e.g., travel delays, weather events, minor aches and pains, and so on), and the results will be the same. They may not be instantaneous, but if you continue to turn things over to the Higher aspect of yourself, then ultimately whatever difficulties you have encountered will fade away. The key is that you

---

[20] Matthew 6:26

must be genuine in your call for assistance, and also willing to see people and situations in a different light.

Acceptance of "What Is" and an Openness to Consider "All Possibilities"

To state it differently, you must drop your perception of how things *should be* and be open to consider all possible solutions. Naturally, the more that you are emotionally tied to your viewpoint, the more challenging it will be to turn things over to your Higher Self. If, however, you are sincere about wanting a solution that is for the highest good of all concerned, then you will – without question – be given one.

The more you practice this process on the smaller issues you face, the easier it will be for you to take on the bigger ones (e.g., money, career, relationships, and the like) that you encounter in your life. This is not to suggest that confronting these larger issues will necessarily be simple; the bigger the problem, the more challenging it usually is for us to "let go and let God." Once again, the key is to *practice* at every opportunity, and recognize that when we fall short we simply have to make our best efforts to do better the next time.

Even as this book was being written, I continued to struggle with some significant issues related to career and financial concerns. In particular, a few times during the nearly five-year period it took to write and produce this book, my longstanding freelance technical writing business effectively ground to a halt. Each time this occurred, no revenue was generated for weeks at a time, and there were also no clear prospects for any new business on the horizon.

Over the years I had faced this type of situation on many other occasions, and by simply remaining calm about it a new opportunity would arise – seemingly out of nowhere – to provide me the sales revenue I needed. Despite these regular demonstrations of abundance, I'd be less than honest if I said that I was totally comfortable moving through these periods of uncertainty.

Rather than succumbing to the fear however, each day I made my best effort to strengthen my faith, and over time, I learned that faith is like a 'muscle'; it must be exercised on a daily basis. This exercise consists of surrendering both our desires and fears to the God-Force, and then trusting in this force that literally created us to assist in manifesting that which we desire.

Now that we've addressed the subject of communicating to God, let's move on to discuss the other half of the equation – the concept of receiving communication *from* God.

COMMUNICATION FROM GOD (INSPIRATION)

Mankind's struggling hard to see the light,
to hear the voice of the Spirit in the night.[21]

TODD RUNDGREN
"NO WORLD ORDER 1.1"

If you tell the average person that you pray on a regular basis, odds are that most would consider your statement to be nothing out of the ordinary. Conversely, if you tell someone that you actually heard a message or received an insight directly from God, it is likely that a majority of those same people will at least doubt what you say; at worst some might think that you could be a candidate for some psychotherapy.

This is primarily the case, because over the centuries many organized religions have made the point that direct communications from God can only be received by those acknowledged to be saintly or very pious individuals. Perhaps the cynicism of some people today can be traced to various televangelists; over approximately the past twenty years many of these folks have made it a practice to use their

---

[21] Todd Rundgren, *No World Order 1.1* Copyright © 1993 by Humanoid Music (BMI) (All rights reserved. Used by permission.) From the CD *No World Order*, (Alchemedia Productions. Manufactured and distributed by Forward, a label of Rhino Records, Inc. 1993).

alleged messages from God to convince people to donate to their ministries. Whatever the reason, it's unfortunate that such widespread skepticism exists about the concept of receiving messages from God, simply because it effectively undermines the willingness of people to give it any credibility.

While it cannot be indisputably proven that each of us gets messages directly from the God-Force, the fact that so many people report receiving Divine communications demonstrates that there is indeed something to this belief. As discussed in Chapter 1, since there is no way of absolutely proving that these alleged communications do or do not actually occur, then one must, at least, acknowledge that it's *possible* that they do. Moreover, it is necessary to leave behind the traditional religious position that only certain people can be conduits for God's messages.

As the previous song lyric from Todd Rundgren indicates, most people, at the deepest level, are longing to hear God's voice, and as this excerpt from Neale Donald Walsch's *Conversations with God, Book 2* illustrates, God makes it very clear that He/She/It is constantly in communication with all human beings:

> *I am giving you guidance every minute of every day. I*
> *Am the still small voice within which knows which*
> *way to turn, which path to take, which answer to*
> *give, which action to implement, which word to*
> *say—which reality to create if you*
> *truly seek communion with Me.*[22]

If we accept the premise that the God-Force is always in communication with us, the key challenge we all face in day-to-day life is one of discerning which of the various messages (i.e., thoughts, feelings) we receive or experience each day actually originate from God

---

[22] Neale Donald Walsch, Conversations with God, Book 2, (Charlottesville, VA: Hampton Roads Publishing Company, Inc., 1997) p. 24

rather than from our ego-mind.

One clear way to determine the source of a message is to take note if there is any fearful thought behind the message. According to the author Sanaya Roman:

> *Messages from your intellect are often based on thoughts of scarcity, guilt, or a need to protect yourself from some imagined threat. The messages from your Higher Self allow you to feel peaceful and balanced. Higher Self-guidance is often subtle and quiet, and is frequently the message that follows the first one you hear.*[23]

It is, therefore, very important to pay close attention to the nature of the feelings, thoughts, and experiences you encounter, particularly when you are in need of some guidance in making a decision. It is also prudent to avoid making decisions based on impulse, since choices made in haste are often driven by your fear-based intellect.

I have found that the most sensible approach when trying to determine the source of an inspiration, is to take a step back from your first impulse, quiet your mind as much as possible, and check your *feelings* about the particular message before taking any action.

God Communicates in Many Ways

There are also instances when God's messages come to us from outside our own conscious mind and feelings. For example, without any personal input, someone recommends a particular book for us to read; or suggests that we go listen to a particular speaker; or we hear a song on the radio with just the right lyric at just the right time.

We then have free-will choice to accept and act on that message, but it is undeniable there was some higher purpose involved in our

---

[23] Sanaya Roman, *Spiritual Growth, Being Your Higher Self*, (Tiburon, CA: H J Kramer Inc., 1989) p. 43

receiving that communication in the first place; there truly are no accidents or coincidences that occur in our perfect Universe.

Many times, God's messages are not oriented towards helping us through a major life issue, but in effect occur in a split-second in response to our need to make a decision. In reality, any time you genuinely ask for guidance in any situation, guidance arrives. You merely need to be open to receiving it, and not locked into a particular course of action, prior to considering your alternatives. For example, if you are driving and aren't sure whether to turn one direction or another, try asking for guidance out loud. If you're truly sincere and open, you will receive an intuition regarding which direction to go.

As stated earlier, it is not usually your first thought, but rather a subtle *feeling* that this way or that way is the best path to follow. Once again, the more you practice asking for help with small issues, the easier it will be to for you to request and then receive guidance regarding the larger ones.

The God-Force also communicates very quickly and clearly to us whenever we encounter a situation that is in some way dangerous, or even life threatening. For example, how many times while driving in your car have you avoided an accident by making a last minute adjustment of some type? If you are an 'average' adult, the answer is probably a number of times. Personally, I have lost count of the number of instances where I have been saved from a potential catastrophe by an instantaneous impulse to change lanes, slow down, or suddenly check my blind spot.

Now, skeptics might say that it is simply one's driving experience that is responsible for such actions, and in some instances they would probably be right. However, what about those situations where the speed of your reaction was so rapid that there literally wasn't enough time for the conscious mind to evaluate the situation and recommend a response? I believe there is simply no other explanation for this other than Divine guidance.

There is yet another way that the God-Force communicates with us, and that is through Nature herself. In particular, according to Native American tradition, the animals and insects that enter and exit our lives everyday offer us guidance and support if we are open to it. This concept is explained in complete detail in a book called *Animal Speak* by Ted Andrews, a truly fascinating work that includes a comprehensive dictionary of animal, bird, and reptile symbolism.

If this material is approached with an open mind, Andrews' work is quite captivating, for it inspires you to pay very close attention to the animals that cross your path on a daily basis, as each one may have a specific message to share with you. Admittedly, it was a bit of a stretch for me to accept this concept in the beginning. The more I referred to this guidebook over time however, it became increasingly obvious that there was merit to it. For example, during one of many times when work on this book had stalled, I was shaving one morning and a spider suddenly appeared right in front of my eyes, suspended from the ceiling on a strand of web.

After the shave was completed, out of curiosity I grabbed *Animal Speak* from the bookshelf to look up *spider*, and that section contained the following information:

> *If spider has come into your life, ask yourself some*
> *important questions. Are you not weaving your*
> *dreams and imaginings into reality?*
> *Are you not using your creative opportunities?*
> *Do you need to write?*
> *Are you inspired to write or draw and not following through?*
> *Spider can teach how to use the written language*
> *with power and creativity so that your words*
> *weave a web around those who would read them.*[24]

After reading those words, a big smile came across my face; I could

---

[24] Ted Andrews, *Animal Speak*, (St. Paul, MN: Llewellyn Publications, 1999) p. 347

not help but be amazed at how appropriate and timely they were. Since that experience, I have made it a practice to be alert to any animals or insects appearing in my life each day, and to always check with the book whenever a new one shows up.

Interestingly, every time I've referred to the book for insight the information provided was highly relevant to something I was experiencing at the time. For this reason, I highly recommend *Animal Speak* as a spiritual growth resource.

From the preceding discussion, it is apparent that the God-Force does communicate with us in a number of ways, and it is our responsibility to be *open* to receive His/Her/Its messages. By maintaining an open mind, we place ourselves in a position to take full advantage of all the loving guidance that is literally always available to us.

MY OWN STORY ABOUT MESSAGES FROM GOD

Back in the early '90s, I was involved in launching a new company from scratch. Things started out smoothly enough, but once egos inflated, conflict developed between my partners and myself. This conflict accelerated to the point where I needed to make a difficult, high stakes decision – one that was very emotionally charged. My body reacted to the stress of the situation until I literally became physically ill from the process. In my heart, I sensed that it was time to move on, but my mind told me to fight it out and win.

One night prior to falling asleep, I recited a brief prayer asking for Divine guidance regarding this challenging situation. Then, in the middle of the night I awoke to this thought that kept repeating in my mind: *"Get on my wavelength and I'll tell you what to do"* – a statement that was very similar to a lyric from a song by my favorite musical artist, Todd Rundgren. I sat up in bed dumbfounded. Was this my answer?

Since I had not heard that particular song for a very long time, I believed that this was indeed the response to my plea for assistance. In that instant, I realized that I needed to drop all of my ego-

centered thoughts and listen to the 'quiet voice' that was telling me
to move on. Within a few days, I chose to heed the advice offered
by that quiet voice, and after nearly fourteen years as a marketing
professional in the personal computer business, I started my own
high tech marketing and writing firm.

As I write this nearly a decade later, I continue to be self-
employed, working part-time from home and enjoying the freedom
associated with being my own boss. And, to think, it all started
with that simple message!

I was so overwhelmed by what happened that night that I spoke with
a spiritually-oriented friend to ask her opinion about what happened.
Her response was that the God-Force knows the best way to communicate to each of us, and in my case it happened to be through song
lyrics. This actually made great sense to me, because from the time I
entered college, the messages held within song lyrics have always capti-
vated me, particularly those that were philosophical in nature.

Interestingly, this insight was not an isolated incident, for since it
occurred I have continued to receive such song lyric-based messages
on a regular basis. These insights usually arrive in the middle of the
night when I'm coming out of a deep sleep, and typically are highly
relevant to some important issue or problem that I am facing at the
time. There have also, of course, been messages that didn't necessarily relate to a specific issue, but nonetheless offered valuable insight
into the nature of life itself.

For example, one time I awakened to this exact lyric from a song
called *Up Where We Belong*:

> *Some hang on to used to be, live their life looking*
> *behind, all we have, is here and now,*
> *all our lives are there defined.* [25]

---

[25] Jack Nitzsche/Buffy Sainte-Marie/Will Jennings, *Up Where We Belong*. Copyright
© 1982 by Warner Chappell Music (All rights reserved. Used by permission. From the
CD *The Essential Joe Cocker*, (Island Records. 1982), (Karussel International, 1995).

The message was very clear to me; I needed to always remember that the present moment is where life is truly lived, where everything we ultimately experience occurs, and that the past is merely a trail we leave behind.

Another message came to me at a time when I was again growing particularly concerned with money issues. In particular, this lyric from a song called *Fight the Good Fight* passed through my mind,

You think a little more money can buy your soul some rest, you better think of something else instead.[26]

That was a very powerful and timely message, one that literally brought tears to my eyes and an 'ah-ha' awareness to my mind.

I could go on and on providing you with a number of other examples, but I am certain you get my point. God's messages can come to us in a host of different ways, and the means of communication used to reach each of us is the perfect one *for* us. As I have stated several times in this chapter, the key to receiving God's messages is to be truly *open* to receiving them. So, make a commitment to being more open-minded, and to paying closer attention to your subtle thoughts and feelings, as well as to the entire world around you.

If you particularly enjoy and are inspired by a certain activity (e.g., reading, running, biking, skiing, listening to music, writing, etc.), then do more of it. And while doing it, be mindful of what goes through your mind or what crosses your physical path; it just might be a message from God!

Summing It All Up

Since the dawn of time, human beings have theorized about the nature and essence of God. Built into our very cells appears to be an

---

[26] Triumph, *Fight the Good Fight*, Copyright © 1981, BMG Careers Music Incorporated (All rights reserved. Used by permission.) From the album/CD *Allied Forces*, (TRC Records. 1981).

insatiable desire to know from whence we came.

From the perspective of many traditional Western religions, God has typically been portrayed as an old white-bearded male in heaven that constantly monitors the Universe, and then punishes His subjects for their sins. This God does not speak directly with His subjects, but only through privileged interpreters who then establish the behavioral ground rules.

A key reason that organized religion remains popular is that each one offers established doctrines and rules to simplify followers' lives. They are then relieved of the responsibility to personally evaluate and contemplate the nature and/or origins of their own existence. However, as Socrates once said, "The unexamined life is not worth living," and therefore it is important to recognize that books like the Bible, Koran, Kabbalah, and others, could, in effect, be collections of stories that may or may not be completely true. There is inherent value within such texts, but it is up to you to discern what information 'feels' right to you in the process of developing your own personal spiritual philosophy.

Throughout history there have been a host of alternative notions about the nature of God, despite the fact that the traditional view of God retains prevalence. One that is quite sensible is the depiction of God as a pure loving *energy* that is constantly creating ideas, items, and circumstances through His/Her/Its creations. This view sees human beings as pieces of this God-Force, not separate from it. Additionally, it recognizes that if God did grant humans free-will choice, then it makes no sense that God would then punish them for breaking 'commandments'. In this view of God, the only real commandment is to *"Love Ye One Another."*

From this author's perspective, all of the stories about a judgmental, punishing God originate from outside our own consciousness, because I believe that we all *know* at a cellular level that God is love, and love alone.

With this view of God, each person is responsible for 'co-creating' his or her life in concert with God. While this concept is incredibly empowering, it also carries with it enormous responsibility, since you can no longer look outside yourself and blame others for your life's circumstances.

Agreeably, this is a radically different way of looking at life than that promoted by conventional religions; once adopted, it opens a person up to criticism from parents and others who remain involved in traditional religious practices. It takes quite a bit of courage to break free from the 'tribe' and follow a new path, but once you make the decision to move forward, you will find yourself begin to attract others who are on a similar path of spiritual discovery.

As you work to develop your own life philosophy, it's a good idea to read and listen to a wide variety of materials related to spiritual growth, and most importantly, to remain open-minded. Ultimately you will know at the *feeling* level what works for you and what doesn't. You'll also acquire a clearer understanding of whether you will be able to successfully integrate any aspects of your traditional religious practice with your new spiritual viewpoint.

This chapter also included a discussion about prayer; it is a common denominator across essentially all cultures. Prayer also tends to be an automatic reaction whenever a person encounters any danger or a life-threatening situation. The use of prayer is taught early in life, and there are literally countless numbers of prayers and a wide variety of prayer methods as well. Although the butt of some jokes in the past, affirmations are also a form of prayer, and they actually do produce desired results if written in the present tense and used on a regular basis.

According to Book 1 of the *Conversations with God* trilogy, the correct prayer is never one of supplication, but rather a prayer of *gratitude*. By thanking God in advance for what you intend to experience in your life, you acknowledge that the seed is planted in consciousness, and as such, already exists *in effect*. Naturally, the key to this approach to prayer is *faith*, which is having such confidence that something will occur that you literally have no doubt about it. That amount of conviction requires that you reach the point where you don't merely *believe* you will experience what you intend to experience, but rather that you *know* you will.

The key to achieving this level of confidence, is coming to the awareness that if the God-Force can manage billions of chemical reactions every minute just to keep you alive, then it can certainly be trusted to assist you in bringing the exact people and/or circumstances into our lives at precisely the right time. To develop that confidence, you simply need to *practice* trusting moment-by-moment, one day at a time, by turning smaller problems over to the God-Force (i.e., your Higher Self) just when you encounter them. As you build up your 'trust muscle', it then becomes increasingly easy to turn the larger issues in your life over to God as well.

Although talking to God is considered commonplace, it is not unusual for people to have doubt whenever someone mentions that they actually *heard* from God. This is primarily because many religions have traditionally stated that only a chosen few individuals have been able to actually hear God's words. It is important to note that while one cannot prove for absolute certain that we all receive messages directly from God, it's also impossible to prove that we do not.

According to *Conversations with God, Book 2*, God is giving us guidance every minute of every day. The challenge for you, then, is to discern which of the thousands of feelings, thoughts, and words passing through your consciousness each day actually originate from God. In that regard, generally the best way to distinguish a Divine message is that it tends to be like a whisper rather than a shout, and it usually follows the first impression you receive. The key is to make best efforts to pay close attention to all of your feelings, thoughts and experiences, and then take some time to reflect on them instead of making your decisions impulsively.

The God-Force also speaks to us immediately whenever we encounter life-threatening situations, and likewise makes an effort to reach us through other people, as well as through books, music, art, nature and even more. Once again, the key to receiving these messages is being open to them, and that tracks back to the importance of maintaining an open mind as discussed in detail in Chapter 1.

If you would but simply begin to make a conscious effort to pay closer attention to the world both within and around you, you will discover that the God-Force is always trying to guide you toward your highest good.

Related Reading

Wayne W. Dyer, *Manifest Your Destiny*: The Second Principle

Stuart Wilde, *The Quickening*: Chapter 11, Spiritual Concepts You'll Probably Never Need

Neale Donald Walsch, *Conversations with God, Book 1*: Chapter 1

Neale Donald Walsch, *Conversations with God, Book 2*: Chapter 2

Neale Donald Walsch, *Conversations with God, Book 3*: Chapter 14

Ted Andrews, *Animal Speak*

Now that we have some additional understanding regarding the nature of God, let's move forward to address another very important subject, namely, just *Who Are You?*

3: Who Are You?

One day soon we'll stop to ponder,
What on Earth's this spell we're under
We make the grade and still we wonder
Who the Hell we are.[27]

STYX
"THE GRAND ILLUSION"

Of the multitude of questions that arise in a person's life, there is little doubt that the most challenging one to find an answer for is, 'Who am I'? It is likely that throughout all of recorded history, this single question has at one point or another at least crossed the mind of virtually every human being that has ever lived.

While some people do seek an answer to this important question, the reality is that most choose to push it out of their minds, for the simple reason that the act of contemplating upon who they really are actually serves to make life even more complicated than it already is! This tendency on the part of mankind to live 'unexamined' lives is what the late Fr. Anthony De Mello was referring to when he said these words:

Most people, even though they don't know it, are asleep.
They're born asleep, they live asleep, they marry in their sleep,
they breed children in their sleep, and they die in their sleep
without ever waking up. They never understand the loveliness and
the beauty of this thing that we call human existence. [28]

The desire to *remain* asleep is quite strong; the fact is that it's much easier to stay focused on the every day world than it is to pay attention to the whisperings of one's soul. The process of *waking up* is very unpleasant for most people, because it requires that an

---

[27] Dennis De Young, Copyright © 1977 by ALMO Music Corp. and Stygian Songs (ASCAP) (All rights reserved. Used by permission.) From the album *The Grand Illusion*, (A&M Records, Inc. 1977).

[28] Anthony DeMello, *Awareness,* (New York, NY: Image Books/Doubleday, 1992) p. 5

individual be willing to seriously question the foundation of his or her entire belief system, including every one of his or her core beliefs about the very nature of existence.

While it may appear easier to just remain asleep, the truth is that avoiding introspection is never beneficial in the long run, for the calling of the soul is very powerful. The more you try to suppress it, the more challenging it becomes to experience true happiness in life. Therefore, the best course of action is to make the effort to wake up, to step outside of your so-called comfort zone, and be willing to explore previously uncharted territory, so that you may ultimately come to an understanding of *who you really are*.

In the balance of this chapter, a number of insights are provided that are intended to help you in this process of stepping outside of the mundane world and discovering your real identity, both from a physical and a spiritual perspective as well.

WHO/WHAT ARE YOU PHYSICALLY?

As you consider this question, you might be thinking, "Come on, I know who I am physically, after all I've been living in this body my entire life." That's not an unreasonable response, but it is not one that gets to the heart of this question: who are you at the *core* physical level? Not what your name is, or what you do or what you look like, but who or what are you at the fundamental level of body?

Your Basic Physical Identity

The simple answer is, that at the basic level you are an unbelievably complex collection of organs, tissues, muscles, fluids, bones, teeth and joints that (usually) all work together flawlessly to keep the 'me' that you think you are alive and functioning. There's nothing earth-shattering in that answer to be sure, but it does provide a segue to the next question, which is, have you ever just for a few moments given *any* thought whatsoever to all of the activities that occur in your body without your conscious involvement?

This excerpt from Deepak Chopra's book *Ageless Body, Timeless*

Mind provides some revealing insights regarding the multitude of events that are taking place within your body, literally every second that you are alive:

> *A hundred things you pay no attention to—breathing,*
> *digesting, growing new cells, repairing damaged*
> *old ones, purifying toxins, preserving hormonal*
> *balance, converting stored energy from fat to*
> *blood sugar, dilating the pupils of the eyes,*
> *raising and lowering blood pressure, maintaining steady*
> *body temperature, balancing as you walk, shunting*
> *blood to and from the muscle groups that are doing the*
> *most work, and sensing movements and sounds*
> *in the surrounding environment—continue ceaselessly.*[29]

In addition to those second-to-second activities, your body is gradually undergoing long-term changes as well. For example, by the end of one year, ninety-eight percent of the atoms in your body will have been exchanged for new ones[30], and by the time seven years have elapsed, your body will have completely replaced itself on a cell-by-cell basis. Amazingly, the stomach lining actually replaces itself every five days, the skin replaces itself once a month, the liver replaces itself every six weeks, and believe it or not, even the skeleton replaces itself every three months![31] And most importantly, all of this occurs without one single bit of conscious effort on your part.

Consider also that every time you eat something, your body automatically takes that food source and breaks it down into its component parts, uses what it needs, and discards what cannot be used as waste. What if you had to consciously control the digestive process?

---

[29] Deepak Chopra, *Ageless Body, Timeless Mind*, (New York: Harmony Books, 1993), p. 13

[30] Ibid., p. 9

[31] Ibid., p. 9

Can you even fathom all of the actions you would need to direct just to digest a single piece of bread? We take so much for granted about our bodies, yet most of us are quick to complain the moment that something within us is not functioning properly.

Genetic Encoded Survival

Your body is genetically coded to keep you alive, and unless you actively do something to inhibit its defenses, it will do everything in its power to preserve your health and life. A great example of this tendency toward perfect health is the body's immediate response to injury. Whenever you cut yourself in a minor way, as you well know, it is simply a matter of moments before the injury begins to heal itself by first clotting the blood in the area, and then immediately beginning to rebuild the damaged tissue.

It is literally remarkable that this myriad of activities is occurring within you at all times, and you effectively have nothing to do with it, as the God-Force is quietly and efficiently taking care of *all* the details. If you pause for a moment right now to think about all of this, there really is no other way to describe your entire physical life as being anything less than an absolute *miracle*. However, how many of us really sit down to appreciate that miracle on a daily basis? Granted it's tough to do that, especially in today's incredibly hectic world, but just the slightest awareness you give to that miracle every day will help to improve your connection with the Divine intelligence that is responsible for that miracle.

Acknowledging the Miracle

To cultivate this awareness of the wonder that you really are, begin right now to acknowledge the miracle that your body is, and the extraordinary activities it performs on a daily basis. For example, make best efforts each day to take a couple of minutes out of your busy schedule to silently thank your body for digesting your food and for removing toxins and waste. In addition, at the end of each day, take some time to express gratitude to your heart for keeping you alive another day, and likewise to all of your other organs, tissues, muscles, bones and joints for their collective efforts on your part.

As you continue with this practice, what you will likely experience is that no matter what the status of your health, you will notice a definite improvement in the way you feel on a physical level. I speak from personal experience regarding this, because for several years now I've made it a daily habit to express such gratitude, and the result has been impeccable physical health, and essentially minimal signs of aging despite moving into my mid-forties at the start of the 21st century.

Naturally there's more to the story, like eating lots of fruits and vegetables, consuming less animal foods, and maintaining a generally active lifestyle. Yet, there exists no doubt in my mind that my daily acknowledgment of the contributions made by every single part of my body plays a key role in keeping me healthy.

I recommend that you adopt the same daily routine of expressing gratitude for each and every part of you, and you may soon find yourself feeling increasingly healthy and more energetic as well. All this providing, of course, that you do not express such gratitude out of one side of your mouth, while simultaneously stuffing the other side with unhealthy food, and sitting idly on the couch most of the time!

WHO ARE YOU AT THE SPIRITUAL LEVEL?

There's a part of me,
That speaks to the heart of me,
Though sometimes it's hard to see,
It's never far from me,
Alive in eternity, that nothing can kill.[32]

JACKSON BROWNE
"THE FUSE"

---

[32] Jackson Browne, *The Fuse,* Copyright © 1976 by Swallow Turn Music and WB Music Corp. (All rights reserved. Used by permission.) From the album *The Pretender,* (Elektra/Asylum Records, a division of Warner Communications, Inc. (now a Time Warner Company) 1976).

As the preceding song lyric so eloquently states, there clearly is much more to each of us than just a body and a personality. This probably isn't news to you, given that you're reading a book about spirituality. However, while virtually everyone on a spiritual path of any sort acknowledges in principle that there is a Higher Self or Inner Being, the vast majority have some degree of difficulty in conceptualizing that aspect of self.

Defining A Higher Self

So what does it mean to have a Higher Self? Does it mean that we are the mortal version of a more advanced being? Does it mean, as many traditional religious texts espouse, that each of us is a lowly sinner that needs to prove ourselves worthy before we can come to know this Divine aspect of ourselves? Or does it perhaps mean that this Higher Self and we are actually one fully integrated entity existing in two separate dimensions?

While these questions cannot be definitively answered by any mortal being, I personally like this description of man's/woman's true nature that appeared in an inspiring book called, *The Quest, A Journey of Spiritual Rediscovery*:

> *We are creations of God. That makes us "children" of God,*
> *and so we resemble God. This is not to say we are God. We are*
> *not God anymore than a wave is the ocean, but the created reflects*
> *the nature of its creator. The wave is born of the ocean—it is a*
> *child of the ocean, and so while it can never be "the ocean", it is*
> *nonetheless one with it. Like the wave, we are expressions of*
> *God's Universe. We are indeed the Universe made alive.*[33]

Almost everyone has heard human beings described as 'children of God', as this terminology is commonly used by virtually all major

---

[33] Richard and Mary-Alice Jafolla, *The Quest, A Journey of Spiritual Rediscovery*, (Unity Village, MO: Unity Books, 1993), p. 49

religions. The traditional religious interpretation of the term 'God's child' is one that connotes, in effect, the typical superior-subordinate relationship that exists between parent and child. In other words, the God-Force is the 'higher-up' and we are the subservient offspring that need to be watched over and disciplined appropriately whenever we step out of line.

In that view, we are not truly one with the God-Force, but instead are separate entities that may be connected to God somehow, but have no real creative power of our own. Instead, we have to *ask* the God-Force to create and provide for us, and that is why most conventional prayers are basically supplications for God to *do* something for the person saying the prayer. By approaching our relationship to the God-Force in this way, we are in essence, as Bob Dylan once said in a song, asking God to serve as our "errand boy" rather than taking any personal responsibility for the manifestation of our desires.

As we learned in Chapter 2, it is more empowering, and – in my view – more accurate to view ourselves as extensions of the God-Force, with the power to attract to ourselves that which we intend to experience. This is *not* to suggest that we are as powerful as the God-Force itself, but what it does mean is that all of us have the ability to access that Universal creative energy, and work in concert with it to make our dreams come true.

Now, if you have grown up with a conventional religious upbringing, it is likely that you have some doubt about your ability to actually work directly with the God-Force to create what you desire in your life. So drop that doubt right this minute, because it doesn't serve you in any way. The reality is that you have indeed created the circumstances of your life through your habitual thinking and feeling patterns.

THOUGHTS ARE THE "CURRENCY OF CREATION"

At the fundamental level then, it is our thoughts that are the true currency of creation. This is because as children of God, we are connected to the God-Force at all times, for it is this higher intelligence that beats our hearts, digests our food, etc. Moreover, our connection to God is not simply physiologically based, but also exists at the level of mind. Our minds truly are extensions of the mind of God, and as such have enormous creative power.

According to Dr. Joseph Murphy:

> *It is the world within, namely your thoughts, feelings and imagery that makes your world without. It is, therefore, the only creative power, and everything you find in your world of expression has been created by you in the inner world of your mind, consciously or unconsciously.*[34]

The preceding passage is just one of perhaps hundreds that could have been referenced regarding the creative power of thoughts. Numerous authors and sages throughout all of recorded history have made comparable statements. And this leads to an important question, which is: what is the nature of our thoughts that gives them such force?

Thoughts as Energy

The simple answer is that a thought itself is at its fundamental level "an impulse of energy and information."[35] More importantly, according to modern quantum theory, those same impulses of energy and information that we experience as thoughts "are the raw material of the universe itself."[36] As such, thought is indeed the most powerful energy in the Universe.

It is also *very* important to point out here that the power of

---

[34] Dr. Joseph Murphy, *The Power of Your Subconscious Mind,* (Englewood Cliffs, NJ: Prentice-Hall, Inc., 1963) p. 24

[35] Deepak Chopra, Creating Affluence, (San Rafael, California: New World Library, 1993) p. 21 Excerpted from *Creating Affluence* by Deepak Chopra © 1993. Used with permission from New World Library, Novato, CA 94949, www.newworldlibrary.com

[36] Ibid., p. 21

thought is even more pronounced with those thoughts we continually focus upon and put *feeling* energy behind, as opposed to those that are more fleeting in nature (i.e., thoughts that come and go and to which we don't normally give much attention).

I have personally come to believe that whatever you concentrate upon with strong emotion is precisely what will manifest in your reality, both the good and the bad. In that regard, consider this highly relevant excerpt from Lynn Grabhorn's practical and very entertaining book, *Excuse Me, Your Life Is Waiting*:

> *It's high time we woke up to the fact that we are electromagnetic beings tripping around with this mindboggling capacity to magnetize into our lives whatever in the world we desire by controlling the feelings that come from our thoughts. There's just no way around it, the way we feel is the way we attract. And more often than not those feelings come from our thoughts, setting up the instantaneous electromagnetic chain reactions that ultimately cause things to happen, to be created, to be withheld, or to be destroyed.*[37]

We human beings are always thinking and feeling, and likewise always creating and attracting, simply because we are constantly sending out these energy impulses, and then taking actions based upon them. The implications of this are quite significant, because it suggests that *whatever* we are focusing on, we are either purposely or inadvertently giving form and substance to it. For example, whenever we seriously *worry* about anything, what we are actually doing is unconsciously using our powerful thought and feeling energy to draw to us what we *don't* want.

Speech as Physical Thought

The same principle applies to our spoken words as well, because speech is simply verbalized thoughts, is it not? This concept is

---

[37] Lynn Grabhorn, Excuse Me, Your Life Is Waiting, (Charlottesville, VA: Hampton Roads Publishing Company, Inc., 2000) p. 13

elaborated upon in this quotation, purportedly channeled directly from Jesus, that appeared in a captivating book called *A New Day Is Dawning*:

> *DO NOT SPEAK WHAT YOU DON'T WANT, because*
> *it is done when you speak it, every idle word. The laws of the*
> *universe do not sift through whether you mean what you say*
> *or intend it to happen. The creative process only puts it in motion.*[38]

This message is very important, for once you come to accept it as truth you cannot help but realize that it's critical for you to become more vigilant about the words you are putting out into the world. Moreover, as this passage from *Conversations with God, Book 1* relates, it is especially important that we not use the words *'I AM'* in front of anything that we don't want to experience:

> *I AM is the strongest creative statement*
> *in the Universe. Whatever you think, whatever you say, after*
> *the words "I AM" sets into motion those experiences, calls*
> *them forth, brings them to you. There is no other way the Universe*
> *knows how to work. There is no other route it knows to take.*
> *The Universe responds to "I AM" as would a genie in a bottle.*[39]

This is a very powerful admonition, for when you stop to reflect on it for a moment, you realize that in normal day-to-day speech it is quite common for all of us to use 'I AM' in some very negative ways. For example, how many times have you heard someone say, "I am depressed, or I am angry, or I am just a klutz," or something similar?

If you are a typical person, it is likely that you've heard or said these types of statements perhaps hundreds of times. In my own case, I commonly used such declarations throughout much of my

---

[38] Diandra, *A New Day is Dawning,* (Naperville, IL: Inward Journey Publishing, 1997) p. 32

[39] Neale Donald Walsch, *Conversations with God, Book 1,* op. cit., p. 93

life until I read *Conversations with God, Book 1* and came across that passage. Since that discovery, I have become far more judicious about how I use the 'I AM' statement in my daily self-talk, and in my conversations with others as well.

So What is This Thing Called "I"?

The previous discussion about using the words 'I AM' leads to another important question, namely, who or what actually is this thing called **'I'**? According to the great spiritual masters, there is no more important question to answer in the entire world.

The key to coming to some sort of understanding of the essence of "I," is to learn to step outside of yourself and literally observe or witness "whatever is going on in you, and around you as if it were happening to someone else."[40] This means that you do not at all personalize what is happening to you; instead you look at things as if you have no connection with them in any respect. If you undertake this approach to observing yourself, what you will notice is something very interesting, because what is actually happening is that *I* is in fact observing *me.*[41]

This refers back to Chapter 1, where I referenced the statement, *"My mind is driving me crazy,"* because it leads to the obvious question, which is, *who* is really making that statement? In response to this inquiry, reflect on this quotation from Fr. Anthony DeMello:

> *We begin first with things, with an awareness, of things; then*
> *we move to an awareness of thoughts (that's the "me"); and*
> *finally we move on to an awareness of the thinker.*
> *Things, thoughts, thinker. What we're really searching for is*
> *the thinker. Can the thinker know himself?*
> *Can I know what "I" is?*[42]

---

[40] Anthony DeMello, *Awareness*, op.cit., p. 46

[41] Ibid., p. 47

[42] Ibid., p. 47

Fr. DeMello then moves on to say that it is actually far more practical to know what the 'I' is *not*:

> *Am "I" my thoughts, the thoughts that I am thinking?*
> *No. Thoughts come and go; "I" am not my thoughts.*
> *Am "I" my body? They tell us that millions of cells in*
> *our body are changed or renewed every minute, so that*
> *by the end of seven years we don't have a single living*
> *cell in our body that was there seven years before. Cells come*
> *and go. Cells arise and die. But "I" seems to persist.*
> *So am I my body? Evidently not! "I" is something other*
> *and more than the body. . . . How about my name?*
> *Is "I" my name? Evidently not, because I can*
> *change my name without changing the "I". . . .*
> *Could we say that "I" is none of these labels we*
> *attach to it? Labels belong to "me."*
> *What constantly changes is "me." Does "I" ever change?*
> *Does the observer ever change? The fact is that no matter*
> *what labels you think of (except perhaps human being)*
> *you should apply them to "me". "I" is none of these things.*[43]

This *'I versus Me'* discussion may seem a bit confusing at first, and if it is, then go back to the beginning of this section and review it, or read *Awareness* by Fr. Anthony DeMello, p. 43–50. The first time I was exposed to this concept, it appeared a bit complicated, but then it all fell into place the more I thought about it.

To clarify this 'I—Me' distinction even further, reflect on this excerpt from E.J. Michael's book *Queen of the Sun*:

> *The 'I' is the kernel of our spirit, the seed of*
> *the immortal I AM PRESENCE. The false self or*
> *'not-self,' what many people call the ego*, is the*

---

[43] Ibid, p. 47–50

> *petty, immature image—or projection—of ourselves,*
> *which masquerades as our real I.[44] (* i.e., the "Me")*

As you gain a better understanding of this concept, you will see that it is simply not appropriate to make a statement like, "I am sad." Instead, it is far more accurate to say something to the effect of, "I am experiencing sadness at this moment," or even "Me is sad," because the plain fact is *you* are *not* your sadness. Notice that this concept also correlates very well to the earlier passage from *Conversations with God, Book 1*, regarding the importance of being careful when using the words 'I AM' in front of any statement.

Once I became aware of the *'I versus Me'* concept, I decided to share it with one of my friends. This individual also saw value in it, and so we ultimately came to an agreement that whenever we communicated with each other, whether verbally or otherwise, we would make our best efforts not to misuse the 'I'. As a result, it was very common for us to have conversations or exchange e-mails with statements like: *"me was feeling very impatient today," or "me is very annoyed at the moment."*

While such language would surely make any teacher of proper English shudder, from a spiritual growth perspective these types of statements are quite simply more accurate, as the higher part of ourselves (the 'I') is incapable of experiencing such thoughts and emotions.

Am I suggesting here that you too follow a regimen such as this in your daily interactions? Yes, and no. *Yes*, that you should be diligent about not using 'I' inappropriately, but of course *no* that you should be required to use 'me' instead of 'I' when communicating either verbally or in writing. However, I do recommend that you make your best efforts to acknowledge in your mind those instances where using 'me' instead of 'I' would have actually been more accurate. Moreover, I strongly suggest that you adhere to the

---

[44] E.J. Michael, *Queen of the Sun*, (New York, NY: HarperCollins Publishers Inc., 1995) p. 171

admonition about not using the words 'I AM' in advance of any statement without first asking yourself this question, *"Is this what I really want to create for myself?"*

SO WHAT ABOUT YOUR "SOUL?"

No discussion regarding who you are would be complete without at least some mention of the word *soul*. It is not my intent here to get into an extensive discussion about the nature of the soul, as a number of excellent books are available that address that subject in detail (e.g., *The Seat of the Soul*, by Gary Zukav, and *Soul Purpose*, by Richard Thurston). In summary though, from all that I have come to understand the soul contains the sum total of each person's thoughts, feelings, and memories from all of their lifetimes here on Earth.

The soul is your entire mind, both the conscious mind, where thinking and reasoning take place, and the subconscious mind, where feelings and memories reside. You are connected to the soul at all times, and it is likewise connected to you. It influences you, and you affect it as well.

REINCARNATION

Now it is quite likely that as soon as some of you saw that word 'lifetimes', a red flag went up in your mind. That is because many people in the West simply will not accept the concept of reincarnation. The primary reason for this is that Judeo-Christian tradition has only flirted with the concept, and has rejected it for centuries even though at an earlier time it was an accepted part of Christian teaching in particular. Additionally, people tend to have problems with reincarnation on a practical level, simply because they cannot understand how they could have lived before but have no memory of it in their current life. In response to that concern, this quotation from a book called *Born Again & Again* by John Van Auken is very illuminating:

*The question crying out for an answer is, "If we have
lived before, why don't we remember it?" The answer is
both simple and complex. The simple answer is, "Because we
have not lived before." This is not completely true, but it is
relatively true because the "you" and "I" that we consider to
be ourselves has not lived before. We think of ourselves
as composed of personality (which includes the conscious mind)
and body. The current conscious mind, personality, and
body are new; they have not been alive before. Nor have
they reincarnated in the true sense of the word.
However, our souls have been alive before—this is
the distinction—and they have reincarnated.
The memories are thus our souls; not ours.[45]*

Relevance of Other Lifetimes to a Current Life

So if we have all lived other lifetimes, this leads to another important question, namely, "What does all of that matter to the life I am currently living?" The short and simple answer is that it matters a great deal, simply because memories from prior lifetimes may actually have a significant impact on our lives today. Ridiculous — some may believe — but ponder on this: How else can you explain that certain fears and behavioral tendencies do not in any way appear related to a person's current lifetime?

For example, how do you account for someone having an intensely powerful fear of flying even though his or her only experience with flight in this lifetime was uneventful? A close relative of mine has missed out on numerous national and international travel opportunities because of it, and cannot at all explain the origins of the fear. Or, how do you explain someone having a spellbinding fear of public speaking, to the point that each time they attempt to deliver an address to a crowd their voice box literally ceases to function? A

---

[45] John Van Auken, *Born Again & Again,* (Virginia Beach, VA; Inner Vision Publishing Company, 1989) p. 98

friend of mine was plagued by this affliction for years, and was unable to trace it to any experience in her existing life.

From my perspective, it's not unreasonable to believe that these fears originated within some other lifetime, and simply were never fully processed/healed by the soul. It is here that the frequently misunderstood concept of *karma* enters. According to John Van Auken once again:

> *Karma is memory coming to consciousness again.*
> *What has occurred in the past is recalled and has an*
> *effect on the present. Now the recollection may not surface*
> *to the conscious level; the personality may have no*
> *awareness of the memory, in fact. Yet it exists at the deeper*
> *soul level. Nevertheless, the soul sees through the same*
> *eyes as the personality, and is reminded of its past use of*
> *free-will and consciousness.*[46]

It is one thing to theorize about past lives, and another thing to actually take some action to uncover information that is relevant to the current life. If you personally are dealing with some fears and/or issues that appear to have no relationship to the experiences of this life, there are individuals that can help you to determine whether past life memories are at the source of them.

Regression Therapy

If your preference is to use a more conventional approach, there are therapists that specialize in regression therapy, a technique that uses hypnosis as the primary means to bring forth past life memories. This therapeutic method is discussed in detail in a book called, *Many Lives, Many Masters* by Dr. Brian Weiss. Published in the early 1990s, the book chronicles Dr. Weiss' surprising transition from a traditional psychotherapist to a past life regression therapist.

---

[46] Ibid, p. 90–91

This change was surprising simply because Weiss had previously never given an ounce of credibility to the concept of past lives. That is, until one day a patient of his by the name of Catherine began relating facts about previous incarnations while under hypnosis. Interestingly, she was able to provide explicit details about individual past lives that were highly relevant to some serious recurring problems that she was encountering in her current life. By going back to observe those lives from a detached point of view, she was able to see her present issues in a different light, and the end result was a complete emotional and psychological healing.

If you are interested in this type of therapy, and are sufficiently open-minded, I recommend that you first read *Many Lives, Many Masters*, and then consider contacting Dr. Weiss by mail to request a referral to an experienced regression therapist in your area. (In addition to Weiss' book, you might also want to read *Journey of Souls* by Michael Newton, Ph.D., as it, too, is an excellent resource in this area.)

Past Life Readings with Psychics/Spirit Channels

If you have no particular preference regarding how you learn about your past lives, then another viable option is to visit a psychic or spirit channel that offers past life channeling sessions. The key to this approach is to identify someone that has demonstrated competence in this area, and that can be quite a challenge given the dearth of *so-called* psychics that exist today. Generally, it's been my experience that the best way to locate a truly gifted clairvoyant is to ask for a referral from friends and associates who are also on a path of personal discovery. These 'word of mouth' referrals are typically very reliable, and arguably much more valuable than conducting a Web search on the word 'psychics' for example.

My Experience with the Awareness of a Past Life

Back in 1996, I came to some knowledge about one of my alleged past lives during a session with a very talented spirit channel that I was referred to by a friend. Candidly, it was not really my intent or interest to explore past lives as I entered this meeting, as I'd always felt that I had enough problems in *this life* without delving into any past ones. This individual explained to me however, that looking into past lives could indeed be a particularly valuable means of gaining insights into the source of chronic issues that crop up in an existing lifetime.

Soon after the session began that day, she shared information with me regarding a lifetime that I apparently lived some centuries ago in a rural village. In that life, at the age of about twelve, I witnessed an attack on my village, one in which the invading tribe looted everything of value, and killed both my parents along with a host of other villagers. According to this individual, the feeling I experienced of losing everything in that life had left a significant karmic impression on me, one that was heavily impacting my current life.

Specifically, at a very deep level I had a fear that everything could be taken away from me at any time, and for that reason I could never relax and fully enjoy that which I did have. As I pondered on that, it occurred to me that it really made great sense, because throughout my adult life I had invested an inordinate amount of mental and emotional energy into monitoring the status of my financial situation.

The lesson that I took from this past life was that it was necessary for me to come to the understanding that in this life I would always have enough, and it was time to begin truly enjoying what I already had. In that regard, it's my pleasure to report that as I write this chapter I'm in the midst of a four-month, unpaid sabbatical from my technical writing business. Without the awareness of that past life issue, there is little doubt in my mind that I would have had the courage to not only forego income for a few months, but also to spend money out of savings as well.

CURRENT LIFE ISSUES AND THE "INNER CHILD"

From the preceding discussion, it should be very apparent that I feel very positively about past life regression therapy, as it has the potential to provide valuable insights into recurring issues that we face in our existing lives. It is important to note however, that the answers to some chronic problems or issues may not be related to a past life at all, but instead may be associated with events that occurred during the formative years (i.e., from infancy through puberty), within our current lifetime.

Healing Your Wounded Child

Psychologists have historically acknowledged how critical these shaping years are in the development of a healthy adult. Proponents of *Inner Child* work in particular, present a strong case regarding the importance of healing the 'wounded' child that reportedly exists in varying degrees within all adults. While there has been some criticism of Inner Child therapy in some circles, I believe the conceptual framework that underlies it is quite sound. In my view the definitive book regarding Inner Child work is the N.Y. Times bestseller called *Homecoming*, by John Bradshaw, but there are a number of other fine books available that effectively address the subject as well.

My purpose here is not to delve into a comprehensive discussion about Inner Child theory, but instead to simply draw your attention to it as a tool that can be used to help you heal current issues or problems that may have originated within your childhood. I personally have done some Inner Child work, and found that it was incredibly helpful to me. As a matter of background, I never thought much of the concept at all, until one day during a meditation session the following thought passed through my mind, "Heal the child, and your life will change."

Like most people I did not pay heed to that message promptly, in fact, I essentially ignored it. Over the next few months however, the same thought kept coming to me until finally one day I went out and bought Bradshaw's *Homecoming*. As I read that book and worked with its various exercises, another thought kept occurring to me, namely that I could really use some help from someone who actually had experience with Inner Child work. Initially, I considered working with a conventional therapist that specialized in this area, but for some reason I did not feel comfortable about taking that path.

Ultimately, I chose to enlist the aid of a clairvoyant person whom I heard had proven experience in doing Inner Child channeling sessions for a number of clients. Interestingly, within just six hour-long sessions, this individual was able to assist me in identifying a series of critical events that occurred during my childhood (ages five through seventeen), that were still affecting me in my forties. Moreover, I was able to see the irrational beliefs and fears that sprung from those critical events, for they were the culprits that led me to behave in many self-defeating ways for so many years. Most importantly, these sessions enabled me to heal many aspects of the child within me that was so deeply affected by those events.

For those of you reading this work that may question the merits of Inner Child work, rest assured that I wholeheartedly understand your concerns. If someone had told me some years ago that I would ultimately participate in such therapy, it's likely I would have gotten really annoyed with him or her. I was the guy that loved that Eagles song *Get Over It*, with its humorous line about taking the inner child and kicking its ass. Yet there I was one day, delving deep into my past to try to make peace with the child that I once was, and which in fact still existed within me. Words cannot fully express how helpful this work was to me, and for this reason I am a strong believer in the value of Inner Child therapy.

WHO YOU ARE NOT!

To close the discussion regarding who you *are*, it is also prudent that we now allocate some time to consider who you are *not*. This is a particularly important topic to me, since for many years I naively felt that who I was, consisted of what I did for a living. Boy, was I ever off base, but in reality I wasn't much different from most of the folks with whom I associated.

Your Profession Is Not Your Identity

In today's world, it's not unusual to equate one's value with one's profession or performance in the working world, but the fact of the matter is, that what you currently do or have done in the past, has absolutely nothing to do with who you really are.

Again quoting Fr. Anthony DeMello:

> *The important thing to do is to drop the labels. . . .*
> *What do I mean by labels? Every label you can conceive*
> *of except perhaps that of human being. I am a human*
> *being. Fair enough; doesn't say much. But when you say,*
> *"I am successful," that's crazy. Success is not part of the "I."*
> *Success is something that comes and goes; it could be here today*
> *and gone tomorrow. That's not "I." When you said "I was a*
> *success," you were in error; you were plunged into*
> *darkness. You identified yourself with success. That same thing*
> *when you said "I am a lawyer, a businessman."* [47]

There is a real danger in strongly identifying yourself with your work or your job, for when the time comes that you no longer do that work, then your identity is effectively lost as well. Put another way, *if what you do is who you are, then when you do it no longer, you will be nobody!* Regardless, today many people tend to be very attached to the status that their employment supposedly provides them.

In particular, how many times have you seen someone lose a long-standing job, and as a result lose his or her sense of self as well? If you're like most people, you have probably seen this occur more than once to friends or co-workers, and perhaps even to yourself. The majority of people tend to work through these times successfully, but there are numerous others who never fully recover from the shock that such a major life change produces.

As an example, I once knew a successful family man who held the

---

[47] Anthony DeMello, *Awareness,* op. cit., p. 73–74

same job as a regional sales manager for more than thirty years. He truly loved the status that was associated with his work, as his management position provided him with nice perks, like a company car as well as other valuable fringe benefits. One day, despite his three decades of experience, this man was abruptly terminated, given a severance package, and promptly shown the door.

As might be expected, the immediate effect of this sudden career change was not – in any way – positive. This individual did not handle the situation well at all. He became so deeply depressed that his family grew very concerned about him. While I'd like to report that he ultimately overcame this career setback, the truth is that at the time this book is being written – eight years later – he still had not. When speaking to his wife one day a few years ago, she shared with me the following information that echoes a point made earlier in this section, "Once Bill lost that job, he truly lost himself, because in his world his job was his whole life, and nothing I can say can convince him to think any differently about what had occurred."

It's easy to view this as a very sad situation, but the reality is that it is by no means unusual, as the majority of people in developed societies tend to strongly identify themselves with their occupation or work. While enjoying and being fulfilled by one's work is certainly important, it is quite another thing to become so identified with that work, that one actually believes that their value as a person is based upon it. Whatever you do for a living is just one of several *roles* that you play in life (e.g., business-person, husband, wife, daughter, son, friend, etc.), and since your work can quickly change, it really has little to do with *who you really are* (i.e., the 'I').

It can be challenging to remember this in today's world, since Western culture is for the most part focused on image rather than substance, and the mass media has done a fine job of glorifying so-called 'social status' and materialism to a worldwide audience. Today, more than ever, you are a success when you have a respected position, earn a certain amount of money, and amass an impressive collection of assets.

This is not to suggest that advancing in one's career and/or becoming financially independent aren't wonderful things to do, because they clearly are. What is inappropriate however, is arbitrarily stating that their achievement is the de-facto definition of success, because success is truly a relative term, is it not? For example, Mother Teresa essentially died without a penny to her name, but throughout the world she would still be considered by most to have been a successful person.

AN ALTERNATIVE VIEW OF SUCCESS

During my twenties and part of my thirties, I fully ascribed to the belief that what I did for a living and what I owned were what defined my success. However, as I read more and more literature related to spirituality and personal growth, it became very clear to me that success really has little if anything to do with achievement or material gain.

In particular, my exposure to the work of Fr. Anthony DeMello had an enormous impact on my entire life philosophy, especially his definition of what it means to be a success, which is summarized in this next passage:

> *Who determines what it means to be a success?*
> *This stupid society! The main preoccupation of society*
> *is to keep society sick! And, the sooner you realize*
> *it the better. Sick, every one of them. They're loony,*
> *they're crazy. You became president of the lunatic asylum*
> *and you're proud of it even though it means nothing.*
> *Being president of a corporation has nothing to do*
> *with being a success in life. Having a lot of money has*
> *nothing to do with being a success in life. You're a success in*
> *life when you wake up! Then you don't have to apologize*
> *to anyone, you don't have to explain anything to*
> *anyone, you don't give a damn what anybody thinks about*
> *you or says about you. You have no worries; you're happy.*

That's what I call being a success. Having a good job or
being famous or having a great reputation has absolutely
nothing to do with happiness or success.
Nothing. It is totally irrelevant.[48]

Even though this was, to say the least, an unconventional view of
success, it made great sense to me from the moment I heard it. The
word 'successful' is merely a label that refers to the 'me' and not the
'I', because success in the traditional sense is actually a fleeting experience. Moreover, once you identify with that success, you're going
to cling to it, and that's when suffering emerges. Why? Because
once you've achieved it, then you feel the pressure to maintain it, or
even enhance it, and the fear of losing it actually serves to prevent
you from really enjoying it!

Living the Fully Aware Life

What Fr. DeMello was attempting to communicate was that true
success is derived from living a fully aware life, one in which you do
not base your happiness on meeting societal standards or acquiring
outside approval.

As a person who spent the better part of thirty years doing the
exact opposite, I can assure you that achieving success in the traditional sense can by no means guarantee happiness. The fact is that
whenever you are *outer* rather than *inner* directed, you can never
truly be in control of your own happiness, for you are in effect a
slave to public opinion. As most people know, this is by no means
an enjoyable space in which to reside, knowing that one moment
you can be up, and then in the wink of an eye you can be down.

Living Independent of Other's Opinions

The way out of this trap of living like a 'yo-yo' is to get to a place
where you can comfortably live your life and make your choices,

---

[48] Ibid., p. 75-76

independent of the good opinion of other people. While most people agree with this advice at a conceptual level, they find it exceptionally challenging to put it into practice on a day-to-day basis. This is because the vast majority of us have been programmed to seek approval from just about everyone *but* ourselves.

It actually starts very early in life, as parents traditionally use approval/lack of approval as important means of controlling a child's behavior. The same type of behavioral control technique is usually employed when the child goes off to school as well. They quickly learn the importance of pleasing their teacher. It is also the most common way to manage the performance of the young adult when he or she completes their education and finally becomes an employee.

Abandoning Your Approval Programming

The good news is that your 'approval' programming can be left behind. It just requires that you become more aware of your need for approval, by using that technique of looking at yourself as if you were someone else. From that vantage point, you can become more cognizant of when your 'me' is feeling the need for approval, and then silently remind yourself that you don't really *need* that person or group to think positively of you. What you actually need is to be true to yourself: first, by not doing things you don't want to do, just to get approval or be liked; second by doing things you enjoy doing, regardless of whether anyone else likes it or not.

"Easier said than done," you might be thinking. But, if you do not choose to pursue this path, the only other option is to continue to please others at the expense of your own happiness. Most people view this as a reasonable compromise, given the importance in most societies of not appearing to be selfish. However, when you continually choose to subjugate your own happiness to make others happy, over time this behavior can lead to some very negative circumstances, including chronic or acute health and/or emotional problems, and ultimately perhaps even an early death.

In the final analysis then, realizing true inner happiness (i.e., your 'bliss') requires that you first come to *truly* know yourself, and second, that you learn to live your life on your terms.

A CLOSING WORD ABOUT SUCCESS

Before leaving this subject, I want to share with you another of my favorite quotations about success, this one from the highly respected Indian Yogi, Paramahansa Yogananda:

> *What is success? If you possess health and wealth,*
> *but have trouble with everybody (including yourself),*
> *yours is not a successful life. Existence becomes futile*
> *if you cannot find happiness. When wealth is lost, you have*
> *lost a little; when health is lost, you have lost something of*
> *more consequence; but when peace of mind is lost,*
> *you have lost the highest treasure.*[49]

At a fundamental level, I believe that what all of us truly want deep within us is peace of mind. What is unfortunate however is that the majority of people choose to look outside of themselves for ways to arrive at this state of mind. In the New Testament of the Bible, Jesus' comment that, "The kingdom of God is within you"[50] suggests to me that only by looking inside ourselves we can come to experience true peace-of-mind. Once you do achieve this state, you'll then clearly know that you are a 'success' regardless of what you do, what you earn, or what you own.

SUMMING IT ALL UP

The majority of people in the world actually spend very little time giving any thought to the age-old question, '*Who Am I?*' Yet living an unexamined life is never advantageous over the long haul, primarily because it requires that you ignore your soul's subtle messages of

---

[49] Paramahansa Yogananda, *The Law of Success,* (Los Angeles, CA, Self Realization Fellowship, 1944) p. 25

[50] Luke 17:21

inspiration and direction.

At the physical level, you are an incredibly intricate assortment of organs, tissues, muscles, bones, and more, that typically work together perfectly and without any effort on your part. Yet, for the most part, few of us take any time on a day-to-day basis to be grateful for the absolute miracle that our body truly is. Nevertheless, by expressing just a small amount of gratitude each day we can move closer to the Divine Intelligence responsible for it.

There is obviously much more to each of us than just a body and a personality. You do have a Higher Self/soul, and you are a child of God, but not a child that is subservient to a demanding Creator. On the contrary, you are an extension of the God-Force, an entity that has the power to work with God to attract to you that which you desire. You may not be as powerful as God, but you do have access to that same creative energy, and you actually make use of it every day. What you must come to realize is that it is you, and you alone, who has created the circumstances of your life through your day-to-day thinking and feeling patterns.

This really should not be a surprise to you, as virtually all great religious and philosophical works have included references to the power of thoughts. Our thoughts are actually the true currency of creation, as these impulses of energy and information are the raw material of the universe itself. We are always creating and attracting via our thoughts, and the implications of this are very important, simply because it means that to whatever we are focusing on with feeling, we are also giving form and substance.

This same principle applies to our spoken words as well, because speech is merely verbalized thoughts. You should be particularly careful about using the words 'I AM' in front of anything that you *don't* want to create, as when these two words are combined they form the most powerful creative statement in the Universe.

According to the great spiritual masters, there is no more important question to answer than "what or who *is* this thing called I?" To answer it, you must learn to step outside of yourself and observe what is going on in you and around you, as if it were happening to someone else. If you do this, you'll soon realize that what is actually happening is that 'I' (the higher part of you) is actually observing 'me' (your ego), and you'll also find that the real you is not your thoughts, but rather you are the thinker behind those thoughts. You'll likewise learn that 'I' is not any of the labels you apply to yourself, except perhaps 'human being', as all of these labels pertain to 'me', since it is only the 'me' you think you are that keeps changing.

Your Higher Self or soul contains the sum total of all of your thoughts, feelings, and memories from all of your lifetimes here on Earth. It consists of both your conscious and subconscious minds, and you are connected to it at all times.

While most people in the West do not accept the concept of reincarnation, many in the East hold to another view, which is that although we have not lived before as this personality, our souls have been alive in other bodies, and the memories of those lives belong to the soul and not to us.

While we do not have immediate access to those soul memories, they can have a significant impact on our lives today. Therefore, the uncovering of past-life memories can be of significant value, and there are two primary ways to accomplish it. First, there are conventional therapists that now specialize in 'regression' therapy, a technique that uses hypnosis as the primary means to bring forth past life memories. Second, there are psychics and spirit channels that offer past life counseling services.

In addition to past lives, your current life can also be significantly impacted by events that occurred during your formative years. Supporters of *Inner Child* therapy in particular emphasize the importance of healing the 'wounded' child that is thought to exist within all adults. While this type of therapy has its share of critics, my personal experience with it was very positive, so I highly recommend it.

In closing the discussion of 'who you are', it is also important to acknowledge that you are not what you do for a living, nor are you what you own. Professions come and go, and money and possessions can be there one day and gone the next. Therefore, labels like 'lawyer' and 'successful' say nothing about the 'I' at all, but instead refer to the 'me'. On this subject, remember this point if nothing else, *if what you do is who you are, then when you don't do it anymore you are nobody!*

This admonition should not be construed to mean that career advancement or financial independence are not wonderful things. It is improper however, to bluntly state that their achievement is the de-facto definition of success, simply because success is a relative term. In the end, achieving true inner happiness is the best definition of success, and this clearly may or may not have anything to do with becoming wealthy or famous.

In the philosophy of Fr. Tony DeMello, a key part of becoming truly happy and legitimately successful is learning to live your life independent of the good opinion of other people. This is very challenging, primarily because most of us have been programmed since birth to seek outside approval, but like anything it can be done with practice. In particular, as you develop your abilities to 'witness' yourself, it becomes easier and easier to recognize when you're seeking approval, therefore enabling you to more promptly put a stop to it.

In the end, experiencing authentic inner happiness and peace-of-mind requires that you acquire detailed self-awareness, and that you learn to live your life on your own terms, regardless of what anyone else thinks.

Related Reading

Deepak Chopra, *Ageless Body, Timeless Mind*: Part One

Richard & Mary-Alice Jafolla, *The Quest, A Journey of Spiritual Rediscovery*: Chapter 4

Dr. Joseph Murphy, *The Power of Your Subconscious Mind*: Chapter 1

Lynn Grabhorn, *Excuse Me, Your Life is Waiting*: Chapter 1

Diandra, *A New Day Is Dawning*: Chapter 4

Neale Donald Walsch, *Conversations with God, Book 1*: Chapter 4

Fr. Anthony DeMello, S.J., *Awareness*: Stripping Down To The "I"; Labels; Obstacles To Happiness

E.J. Michael, *Queen of the Sun*: Chapter 9

John Van Auken, *Born Again, And Again*: Chapters 7 & 8

Alan Cohen, *Dare to Be Yourself*: Dare to Respect Yourself

Paramahansa Yogananda, *The Law of Success*: Success Is Measured by Happiness

John Bradshaw, *Homecoming* (SB: Inner Child)

In Chapters 2: *Who or What is God?* and 3: *Who Are You?* I have made an effort to bring greater simplicity to what are clearly two very complex subjects, and from here we move on to do the same with six spiritual principles. The first of these, *Cause & Effect*, is discussed in Chapter 4.

4: Cause and Effect

*Go on pretending
you don't know the ending.
All the things you weren't intending,
but your broadcast continued sending.*[51]

TODD RUNDGREN
"PROACTIVITY"

The principle of *Cause and Effect* is more commonly known by the axiom "what you sow is what you reap," and is also referred to by the slang saying, "what goes around, comes around." It essentially means that every *effect* that you see or experience in the world had to have a *cause*. While at first glance this may appear to be a very simple and obvious concept, it has profound implications for every human being. What it means is that literally every single thought and feeling you experience is a cause that sets into motion an eventual effect. This insightful passage from Lynn Grabhorn builds upon this point:

> *Every time we think of anything, we're flowing some
> kind of positive or negative energy (feeling) toward whatever
> it is we're thinking about, and the litany never changes:
> as we think, we feel; as we feel, we vibrate; as we vibrate,
> we attract. Then we get to live the results.*[52]

It is critical that you comprehend the importance of this principle, for once you do, you better position yourself to realize your full potential for both personal and spiritual growth. At its most fundamental level, this principle states that the Universe is in fact a very

---

[51] Todd Rundgren, Copyright © 1993 by Humanoid Music (BMI) (All rights reserved. Used by permission.) From the CD *No World Order*, (Alchemedia Productions. Manufactured and distributed by Forward, a label of Rhino Records, Inc. 1993).

[52] Lynn Grabhorn, *Excuse Me, Your Life Is Waiting* op. cit., p. 46

sensitive energy field, and that whenever we make a choice to think, feel, speak or act in a certain way, we are emitting energy into this field that must return to us in comparable form.

CAUSE AND EFFECT AS A BOOMERANG

Put another way, the principle of cause and effect serves as our own personal 'boomerang', meaning it's very important that we make our best efforts to toss that boomerang out into the Universe with positive energy attached to it, for whatever we put out there will assuredly return to us in kind. According to Arnold Patent in his book, *You Can Have It All*:

> *Energy flows out of our bodies like a signal or*
> *wavelength from a radio or television station. Each of us*
> *emits a very precise signal. Everyone and everything in*
> *our environment picks up certain of these signals. However, only*
> *those who are on the same wavelength respond to them. . . .*
> *The result then is that we attract into our lives those people*
> *and those circumstances, which are in alignment*
> *with the energy signals we emit.*[53]

Given the above premise, it is reasonable to conclude that everything that happens to us originated with a cause that we *ourselves* set into motion. The problem that most people have with this principle, however, is that they simply cannot understand how some *effects* can happen to them when they cannot consciously recall doing anything to *cause* them.

From all that I've read, it is my understanding that not all of our choices are made at the conscious-mind level, as over time all of us develop conditioned (i.e., subconscious) responses to a variety of stimuli. It can also be true that a cause set into motion in one area

---

[53] Arnold M. Patent, *You Can Have It All*, (Piermont, NY: Money Mastery Publishing, 1984) p. 42

of life, may actually have its effect in an entirely different area, making it challenging for people to connect them.

SPIRITUAL GROWTH REQUIRES
MORE CONSCIOUS DECISION-MAKING

One of the keys to spiritual growth therefore, is learning to discipline yourself to become more conscious about all of the decisions (i.e., choices) that you do make. In his book *The Seven Spiritual Laws of Success*, Deepak Chopra has some excellent advice regarding this:

> *When you make any choice—any choice at all—you can ask yourself two things: First of all, "What are the consequences of this choice that I am making?" In your heart you will immediately know what these are. Secondly, "Will this choice that I'm making now bring happiness to me and to those around me?*[54]

As you begin to put this advice into practice, you'll be amazed at how many of your thoughts, feelings, and actions have been occurring on 'auto-pilot', so to speak. Over time we all become so conditioned, in both our thinking and in our behavior, that we really don't take the time to look upon the everyday situations we encounter in a new light. This is because our subconscious mind effectively operates as a powerful supercomputer, one that instantly evaluates any stimuli we encounter against its vast 'memory bank', to determine if we have experienced something comparable to it in the past.

To make your choice making a more conscious experience, you must – in a sense – 'short-circuit' the subconscious mind, and undoubtedly this requires some effort on your part. While initially you may find it quite challenging to bring more of your choice making to the level of consciousness, with practice you will find it

---

[54] Deepak Chopra, *The Seven Spiritual Laws of Success*, (San Rafael, CA: Amber-Allen Publishing & New World Library, 1994) p. 42

increasingly easy to do so. Your objective should be to become as conscious as possible regarding all of the choices that you do make. However, given the myriad choices that you make on a daily basis (e.g., thoughts, words, actions), it is only natural that you will continue to make a number of them on a subconscious level.

My recommendation is that you not drive yourself crazy with this, rather just make your best efforts to develop personal *awareness* of the various choices that you are making, by learning to step back and witness them (i.e., from the perspective of the 'I') as you make them. Through this simple act of witnessing, you actually take the entire process from the unconscious realm into the conscious realm. Finally, throughout this process always remember to have patience with yourself, for as the old adage goes, "Rome wasn't built in a day."

WHAT ABOUT PAST CHOICES?

Moving toward more conscious choice- making is clearly in your best interests, but it also raises another very important question, which is this: what if anything, can be done about all of the choices that you have already made on an unconscious basis? To say the least, it is a bit unnerving when you stop to think about all the causes you may have initiated in the past (i.e., from this lifetime and even past lifetimes), that could ultimately emerge as some type of negative effect.

You could easily become quite fearful about such things, yet you must also remember that there could be a variety of *positive* effects that might show up as well. As for those of a negative nature that may be lurking about, there are a couple of constructive actions you can take to lessen the impact they might eventually have on your life. First, as this next passage indicates, you can recognize that in each new moment you have the golden opportunity of initiating *new causes*:

> *While it's true that every cause you have set into motion will eventuate in a corresponding effect,*

don't start looking over your shoulder for your
past to catch up with you! Know why? Because you can
always put a new cause into motion. That should be a
comforting thought, considering all of the foolish
things you may have done in the past. . . . If you are
dissatisfied with a part of your life, know that it is the
effect of a cause that you have put into motion and
that at any time you can start again.
Your new cause will bring a new effect.
"The measure you give will be the measure you get." [55]

Reframing Negative to Positive

The other step that you can take is to reframe or transform the negative effect into a positive one. In particular, as you are going through the negative event or circumstances, ask yourself, "What am I supposed to learn from this?" or "What message is the Universe trying to convey to me through this experience?" As you quiet your mind and listen for a response to those types of questions, you are demonstrating to the Universe that you are aware that all problems contain the seeds of opportunity, and that you are willing to see the underlying value in what you are experiencing.

The first time I tried to apply this approach in my life was right after the failure of my first entrepreneurial venture back in 1991. Whereas in the past, I normally would have been complaining and lamenting my fate, I instead adopted the attitude that there was obviously something I needed to learn from that experience. As I carried this attitude forward, I discovered that it was much easier to handle the setback.

Why? Because rather than blaming, I was accepting responsibility (at some level) for my part in what had occurred. Moreover, I was able to gather some very important insights into why the experience

---

[55] Richard and Mary-Alice Jafolla, *The Quest, A Journey of Spiritual Rediscovery*, op. cit., p. 93 - 94

happened in the first place. If you, too, adopt this approach of sincerely asking "What's the lesson?" rather than "crying the blues," I assure you that the Universe/God-Force will provide you with the information you need to come to a clearer understanding of the deeper meaning behind whatever it was that you experienced.

TAKING FULL RESPONSIBILITY FOR YOUR LIFE

As you embrace the concept that it is *you* that causes the effects you experience in your life, then by logic it's obvious that you are responsible, at some level, for everything that happens to you. This is a challenging concept for most people to accept, because as mentioned earlier, it means that we are even responsible for all of the negative things that happen to us. For example, if you are beset by a critical illness that comes upon you seemingly without warning, it can be quite difficult to accept that at some level *you* caused it.

You Create Your Life

Nevertheless, adopting the mindset that you do indeed cause/create *all* of the circumstances you experience in life, even if you don't recall doing so consciously, opens the door to the potential for greater joy by removing you from the backwards-focused paralysis of blame. It also transports you into the now moment of *responsibility* where you can actually take action to resolve problems and issues. In that regard, I will never forget the following statement made during a presentation by a gifted motivational speaker named Brian Tracy: "Blame looks backward; responsibility is today."

What a simple yet powerful concept! Either you accept responsibility, which is focused in the present moment where solutions can actually be identified and implemented, or you stay mired in the past by pointing the finger of blame at other people, at yourself, at God, etc.

In the past, when I worked in conventional corporate positions, like most people blame was a regular part of my survival repertoire, since it was so much easier to do than taking responsibility. Now as I reflect on those days, it is very obvious that blaming serves no purpose at all, other than to stall the progress in solving a particular problem.

Without question, my favorite quotation related to the importance of taking full responsibility for our lives is the following one that is found in a book called *A Course in Miracles*:

> *I AM responsible for what I see. I choose the feelings*
> *I experience, and I decide upon the goal I*
> *would achieve. And everything that seems to*
> *happen to me I ask for, and receive as I have asked.*[56]

When I first read those words I was a bit taken aback. In all honesty the premise behind this passage was very foreign to me. Yet, the more I pondered it, the more it made sense to me, particularly in light of the principle of cause and effect. If one accepts the essence of this principle, then it isn't difficult to agree with the proposition that we actually do have a direct hand in causing/creating (either consciously or unconsciously) those things that we experience in our lives.

More importantly, by coming to this awareness, we can rise to a new level of empowerment, because now we truly know that to have different *effects* manifest in our lives, we quite clearly have to become more conscious about the various choices that we make each and every day of our lives.

SUMMING IT ALL UP

The principle of cause and effect essentially states that every *effect* that you see or experience in the world had to have a *cause*. On the surface it's a simple concept, but as you look closer you come to understand its significance. What it actually means, is, that literally every single one of your thoughts, feelings, words and actions is itself

---

[56] Foundation for A Course in Miracles, Inc.®, *A Course in Miracles,* (New York, London: Penguin Books, 1975), p. 448

a cause that invariably sets into motion a corresponding effect.

From all that I've learned, at a fundamental level the Universe is in reality a highly sensitive energy field, and whenever you make any choice at all, you actually emit energy into it. *The bottom line, therefore, is whatever you put out into the world is what you'll get back someday, so you need to be very careful about what it is that you're putting out there.* The problem that most people have with this principle is that they cannot recall creating the cause that led to a particular event. However, not all choices are made consciously, as each of us develop conditioned responses to various stimuli, plus the causes we put out there in one area of our life may actually lead to effects in a completely different area.

One of the keys to spiritual growth therefore, is learning to become a more 'conscious' choice maker. This requires that you take the time to evaluate every choice you make so as to fully identify its potential consequences. This takes a lot of practice, and because of the sheer number of choices you make each day, there will of course be choices that you'll continue to make on a subconscious basis. So at a minimum, just do your best to develop an *awareness* of the various choices that you are actually making each day.

Do not be overly concerned about the causes you've unconsciously put out there in the past, because some of them may actually lead to positive effects. As for potential negative effects, there are some practical actions you can take to lessen the impact they may ultimately have on your life. In particular, you always have the option of putting a new, more empowering cause into motion, and you can also reframe the situation by choosing to view any negative effect as a learning experience.

Once you accept the validity of the principle of cause and effect, the next step is for you to acknowledge that you are indeed responsible for everything that you ultimately experience. As you come to this awareness, you can then stop blaming (an activity focused on the past) and instead move into the *now moment* of responsibility, which is the only place where problems can actually be solved. When you decide to make this shift in your internal perspective, you will rise to a new level of empowerment in your life.

Related Reading

Lynn Grabhorn, *Excuse Me, Your Life is Waiting*: Chapter 2

Arnold Patent, *You Can Have It All*: Cause and Effect

Deepak Chopra, *The Seven Spiritual Laws of Success*: Chapter 3

Richard & Mary-Alice Jafolla, *The Quest, A Journey of Spiritual Rediscovery*: Chapter 8

Foundation for A Course in Miracles, Inc., *A Course In Miracles*: Chapter 21

In the next chapter, we will explore the vital principle of *Present Moment Awareness*.

5: Present Moment Awareness

Some, hold on to used to be,
Live their lives, looking behind,
All we have is here and now,
All our lives, are there defined.[57]

JOE COCKER W/JENNIFER WARNES
"UP WHERE WE BELONG"

The essence of the *Present Moment Awareness* principle is that the only time that is real is in the present, for it is from within the now that everything we experience in life springs. This principle clearly opposes what most of us have been taught in the western part of the world, where what did happen or what may happen virtually always gets far more attention than what *is* actually happening.

According to author and sage Eckart Tolle:

Have you ever experienced, done, thought, or felt
anything outside the Now? Do you think you ever will?
Is it possible for anything to happen or be outside the Now?
The answer is obvious, is it not? Nothing ever happened in the
past; it happened in the Now. Nothing will ever happen in
the future; it will happen in the Now. What you
think of as the past is a memory trace,
stored in the mind, of a former Now.
When you remember the past, you reactivate a
memory trace—and you do so now. The future is an
imagined Now, a projection of the mind. When
the future comes, it comes as the Now.
When you think about the future, you do it now.
Past and future obviously have no reality of their own.[58]

---

[57] Jack Nitzsche/Buffy Sainte-Marie/Will Jennings, *Up Where We Belong*. Copyright © 1982 by Warner Chappell Music (All rights reserved. Used by permission. From the CD *The Essential Joe Cocker*, (Island Records. 1982), (Karussel International. 1995).

[58] Eckhart Tolle, *The Power of Now*, (Novato, CA: New World Library, 1999), p. 41 Excerpted from *The Power of Now* by Eckhart Tolle © 1999. Used with permission from the New World Library, Novato, CA 94949, www.newworldlibrary.com

If you honestly take the time to step back and witness your thoughts for, say a five or ten-minute period, you will be shocked to find that the vast majority of them actually have nothing to do with the present moment at all.

LIMITED AWARENESS OF THE 'NOW'

The truth is you actually spend very little time being fully aware of what is occurring in any given moment. If you are like most people, your mind is always trending towards thoughts about the past (i.e., regrets, anger, reminiscing), or thoughts about what may or will occur (i.e., worries, anticipated events).

The present is real simply because it is the only time that your total being (i.e., mind and body) actually *experiences*. Ponder on this for a moment: "Is your body ever physically in the past or the future when you're thinking about either of them?" The answer is of course a resounding *NO*, which makes it very obvious, that any time other than the present exists solely *within your mind*. So, as your mind continues its habit of wandering both forward and backward, you are obviously not taking full advantage of the only worthwhile time you actually do have.

PROBLEMS TYPICALLY RELATE TO THE PAST & FUTURE

If you traced all of your problems to their sources, you would likely find that they are virtually always related to something in the past or in the future. Therefore, the more attention you give to them, the less energy you have available for use in the 'here and now'.

So, why is it that our minds are so easily distracted from being in the present moment? The simple answer is that our lower self (i.e., the ego, or 'me') has, for the most part, been conditioned to feel guilty, remorseful, or angry about the past, and insecure or fearful about the future.

Guilt, for example, is regularly used in the socialization process as a means of controlling behavior in the present; for example: *How could you have hurt me in this way after all I've done for you?* As for

the future, from the time we were kids, our parents, as well as society in general, continually filled us (and still do) with fear about all of
the negative things that *could* happen to us.

A CLOSER LOOK AT "THE PAST"

As an exercise, stop for a moment right now and think of something that happened in your past that you still carry some regrets
about. Perhaps it's a failed relationship, a job that you lost, a business that failed or a business you failed to start, an accident you
either caused or one that affected you, etc. You can also complete
this exercise by thinking back to something pleasant that you experienced, such as falling in love, getting a promotion, or having a wonderful time on vacation.

Whether what you experienced was positive or negative, as you get
in touch with that event or set of circumstances, realize that what
you are doing in effect, is time-traveling within your own mind as
you search through your bank of memories.

The Past Is Only An Illusion

The truth is that the past is merely an illusion, as it is only what
your mind is able to selectively remember. Moreover, the longer
something remains in the mind, the more it changes and the less it
reflects what may have actually occurred.

The bottom line is that all you really have is your perception of
what happened, and it is not necessarily clear, since the lens you are
looking through may actually be clouded by the emotions associated
with that memory. In addition, as referenced above, your memories
tend to change over time, and therefore may not accurately reflect
your original perception. Despite this, the average person spends a
great deal of time in this illusionary world of the past, either feeling
guilty, regretful or angry, or reminiscing about the so-called "good
old days".

Remorse, Regret, and Forgiveness

If you find yourself feeling remorseful about something you have said or done, or regretting something you feel you should have done, what you must do is learn to *forgive yourself.* By this I mean that you literally need to look at yourself in the mirror and say with conviction, "I forgive you for the mistake(s) you made, since I now know that you were simply doing the best that you were capable of doing at that time." It is likewise important for you to acknowledge that everything that ultimately did occur was a necessary part of your soul's growth.

What you also need to do when you are feeling guilty isn't necessarily to apologize to whomever you hurt or disappointed, but instead to acknowledge your commitment to never repeating the behavior again. This is not to say that you shouldn't make an apology for something if you feel compelled, rather, that it is more important to avow that you have actually *learned* from your mistake.

Accepting Responsibility Negates Anger

If you feel angry about something that occurred to you in the past, stop and internally remind yourself that according to the principle of cause and effect, it was *you* who initiated the cause, either consciously or unconsciously, that led to the effect that incited your anger. By adhering to this view you effectively prevent yourself from becoming a powerless victim of circumstances.

While it can be very challenging to adopt this perspective, once you do it becomes nearly impossible to get angry at anyone for more than just a brief moment. Instead, you learn to look for the deeper meaning or a lesson behind each of the troublesome situations that you encounter, and learn to silently honor those individuals who can 'pull your strings', for they are serving as valuable teachers. Moreover, make an effort to remember that these annoying individuals are providing you with valuable opportunities to practice remaining centered in the midst of turmoil.

Reminiscing is Non-productive

If you tend to reminisce about good times or relationships you have experienced in the past, you must understand that these types of thoughts also keep you from fully experiencing the present moment. Ideally, what you need to do is to develop the ability to completely experience whatever it is you're experiencing at any given time, and then leave it behind. In the words of Fr. Anthony DeMello:

> *Don't carry over experiences from the past. In fact, don't carry over good experiences from the past either. Learn what it means to experience something fully, then drop it and move on to the next moment, uninfluenced by the previous one. You'd be traveling with such little baggage that you could pass through the eye of a needle. You'd know what eternal life is, because eternal life is now, in the timeless now.*[59]

Although this may seem like novel advice, it is quite practical, because many of us have a tendency to, as Henry David Thoreau once said, "loiter in winter when it is already spring." If you are a person that is inclined to focus on good times in the past, please understand that all you are doing by 'time-traveling' in this way is wasting thought and feeling energy that could be used in far more constructive ways. If you can begin to put into practice even in a small way what DeMello is recommending, you would most certainly notice an improvement in the quality of your life. You would also come to realize that *these* are indeed "the good old days."

Wasting Energy on that which is Over & Done

The past only has an impact on the present when you continue to waste your powerful thought and feeling energies on something that no longer exists at all, other than in *your own mind*. Whatever it was that happened is finished now, and no matter how uncomfortable it

---

[59] Anthony DeMello, *Awareness,* op. cit., p. 132

was for you, you need to come to the understanding that at some level you chose it, and that it helped to build your character and make you a stronger individual.

Whenever you do find yourself wondering why something turned out the way it did, I suggest calling to mind the old adage that often times 'God does work in mysterious ways'. The truth is, you really don't know the "big picture." So, even though you might be inclined to feel sad about a certain event in your past, make the decision to accept the realization that there is a higher order to things, and that something good will eventually come of it.

Your Past Doesn't Have to Drive the Present

Before leaving the subject of the past, I want to share with you a thought-provoking analogy I have heard Dr. Wayne Dyer use on more than one occasion during live presentations. The analogy is this: when you believe that the past has a significant, if not irre-versible effect on your life today, it is just like saying that when a boat moves across the water, it is being propelled by the wake behind it. Naturally this is ridiculous, because everyone knows that the wake is the result of the boat's forward movement through the water and nothing else. The reality is, your past doesn't drive your boat in the present moment, you do!

A CLOSER LOOK AT "THE FUTURE"

What I am about to say may shock you, but other than those times when you are looking forward with joyful anticipation to an upcoming event, practically all of the thoughts you entertain about the future are in fact rooted in *fear*. In particular, the desire to know what will occur, and the urge to make detailed plans to ensure one's own security down the road, are both related to the ego/the 'me's' need for safety as a result of its deeply held fear of death.

You can deny the truth in this, arguing that it is only prudent that a person plan for the future. However, if you are able to look deep within yourself, you will realize that it is indeed an accurate observation concerning human nature. To varying degrees, every single one of us is apprehensive about the future (i.e., the unknown), and so we burn amazing amounts of energy trying to get a hold on something that quite simply is impossible to grasp. According to Fr. Anthony DeMello:

> *So why are you anxious? Can you, for all your anxieties,*
> *add a single moment to your life? Why bother about tomorrow?*
> *Is there a life after death? Why bother about tomorrow?*
> *Get into today. Someone once said, "Life is what happens to us*
> *while we're busy making other plans." That's pathetic.*[60]

These certainly are powerful words, and yet it is really tough to challenge DeMello's observations. Think about it carefully for a moment or two. What possible benefit can be derived from feeling anxious about the future? The answer is none, unless of course you happen to enjoy experiencing the feeling of anxiety. Moreover, what is the payoff for spending a great deal of time planning one's life in minute detail? Perhaps all of this preparation helps people to assuage their fear of the future to some extent, but it quite obviously prohibits them from truly enjoying their present moments.

Plan for the Future or Focus on the Present?

In truth, detailed planning for the future is not nearly as important as learning to keep your powerful thought and feeling energy concentrated in the present. The key to having the future you want is to clearly set your intent today, and then make your best efforts to focus thoughts and feelings each day on what you *do want* rather than what you *don't want*. This sounds like simple advice, yet most people are inclined to let their fears get the better of them, and subconsciously allocate more of their "currency of creation" (i.e., thoughts and feelings) toward concerns about *not* getting what they want.

---

[60] Ibid., p. 114

Getting out of this trap is very challenging, because the ego's desire for security is so strong that your mind tends to automatically gravitate toward 'future-thought'. From my own experience, a key to freeing yourself from this tendency is to work towards becoming a conscious *observer* of your thoughts. Once again, this means cultivating the ability to step back and acknowledge your thoughts as they crop up, and then doing your best to give the minimum amount of energy to those that are based in fear. As with any skill we work to develop within ourselves, remember to be patient with yourself, and also keep in mind the old adage that "practice makes perfect."

One rather thought-provoking way to overcome our inclination toward 'future-thought' is described in this additional quotation from Fr. Anthony DeMello:

> *Visit a graveyard. It's an enormously purifying and*
> *beautiful experience. You look at this name and you say, "Gee,*
> *he lived so many years ago, two centuries ago; he must have*
> *had all the problems that I have, must have had lots of sleepless*
> *nights. How crazy, we live for such a short time.*
> *An Italian poet said, "We live in a flash of light; evening comes,*
> *and it's night forever." It's only a flash and we waste it.*
> *We waste it with our anxiety, our worries,*
> *our concerns, our burdens.*[61]

The next time you find yourself concerned with the future, visualize yourself looking down at your own tombstone, lamenting about how much time you squandered worrying about what might happen *someday*. The question is, do you really want to experience such feelings of regret after you depart this earth? Of course you don't! So one thing you can do when you find yourself feeling fearful or anxious about the future is to recall that image of your own gravestone, and use it as a reminder to keep your thoughts focused in the present moment.

---

[61] Ibid., p. 170

Overcoming Concerns about the Future

Taming one's trepidation about the future ultimately requires that a person muster up the courage to face up to his or her fears. What you will find as you embark upon this course is that it is kind of like confronting the neighborhood bully when you were a kid, in that those fears are not nearly as intimidating as you thought they would be.

Before leaving this discussion of 'the future', I will share with you another insightful quotation from *The Quest, A Journey of Spiritual Rediscovery* by Richard and Mary-Alice Jafolla:

> *What about the future? Can you believe that if you*
> *keep on thinking the same thoughts, saying the same words,*
> *doing the same things, going in the same direction,*
> *the future will be any different than now?*
> *To look to the future as a savior without changing*
> *the present is to think*
> *an orange tree can grow from an acorn.*[62]

Each moment of your life you have the unique opportunity to plant new seeds of thought, seeds that have the potential to someday sprout into all that you desire. In light of this reality, do not waste time fretting about what *may* occur, rather make full use of all of your 'now' moments by choosing to consciously *create* your ideal future instead.

STAYING IN THE PRESENT MOMENT

Learning to be fully in the present is a skill that requires constant practice, because as you well know, your mind has strong tendencies to migrate both forward and backward. The key to mastering this skill is to regularly remind yourself of the importance of truly focusing on what you are doing or experiencing 'right now'.

---

[62] Richard and Mary-Alice Jafolla, *The Quest, A Journey of Spiritual Rediscovery*, op. cit., p. 280–281

As Dan Millman so eloquently says in his book *The Laws of Spirit*:

> *Embrace this moment, put one foot in front of the other,*
> *and handle what's in front of you. Because no matter*
> *where your mind may roam, you body always remains*
> *here and now. When in haste, rest in the present.*
> *Take a deep breath, and come back to here and now.*[63]

This, of course, requires some conscious effort on your part, but over time you will get more and more adept at it. To help you develop this skill, I have found that it is a good idea to create a simple reminder phrase such as "am I fully in the present?" and paste it up in conspicuous places within your house (e.g., a bathroom mirror or refrigerator). You can even place one somewhere within your workspace at the office, and on your car dashboard. At first glance this may appear to be a bit silly, but I can assure you from personal experience that it does help to keep you more focused in the 'now'.

Being More Attentive to Sensory Input

In addition to learning to be more mentally focused in the present, it is also important to train yourself to pay greater attention to all of the sensory input that your body is receiving in any given moment. For example, listen to *all* the sounds that you can detect around you, look closely at what you are seeing, fully breathe in all of smells you encounter, and truly touch what you are touching. As you pay greater heed to your five senses, you automatically move into the *now* simply because those senses are part of your body, and, as stated earlier, the only place your corporeal body can be is 'here and now'.

Becoming more sensory-aware requires a strong, conscious effort on your part because your brain automatically functions to channel all of the information it receives into a very narrow bandwidth. The brain completes this filtering process so that you do not have to

---

[63] Dan Millman, *The Laws of Spirit*, (Tiburon, CA: H.J. Kramer, Inc., 1995) p. 40

concern yourself with consciously sorting through tons of sensory data. While there are obvious benefits to this, the drawback is that you become less and less aware of all that is going on around you.

To overcome this, as stated on the preceeding page, it is necessary that you train your mind to begin to notice as much as possible. For example, when walking down a street, instead of just looking right in front of you, practice scanning from side to side to overhead, making sure to observe everything with as much detail as you can. If you see a bird, don't think, "Oh, there's a Robin," but rather learn to see it as the unique creature that it truly is. In addition, once again be aware of any of the smells that you encounter, and each of the sounds you hear as well. By sharpening your sensory awareness in this way, you will find yourself living more and more fully in the present moment.

Before moving on to the next chapter, I will close the subject of present moment awareness with this insightful passage from Neale Donald Walsch that appeared in *Conversations with God, Book 1*:

> *There is no such thing as 'getting to heaven.'*
> *There is only a knowing that you are already there.*
> *Enlightenment is understanding that there is nowhere to go,*
> *nothing to do, and nobody you have to be*
> *except who you're being right now.*
> *You are on a journey to nowhere.*
> *Heaven—as you call it—is nowhere.*
> *Let's just put some space between the w and the h*
> *in that word and you'll see that*
> *heaven is now ... here.*[64]

SUMMING IT ALL UP

The principle of *Present Moment Awareness* states that the only time that is *real* is in the present, for it is from within the 'now' that

---

[64] Neale Donald Walsch, *Conversations with God, Book 1*, op. cit., p. 98

everything we experience in life originates. The present is 'real' simply because it is the only time that your total being (i.e., mind and body) experiences. The primary reason we are pulled out of the present is that our lower self (i.e., 'me') has been conditioned to feel guilty, remorseful, or angry about the past, and insecure or fearful about the future.

Whenever you do choose to drift into thoughts about the past (either positive or negative), what you are effectively doing is time traveling within your own mind. The past is only an illusion, for it is merely what your mind is able to selectively recall, and is in reality only your perception of what occurred. Regardless, the average person spends a great deal of time in this illusory world of the past, either feeling guilty, angry, or contentedly and unproductively reminiscing about the so-called "good old days".

When you are feeling remorseful, the first thing you need to do is to forgive yourself, for you were simply doing the best you knew how to do at the time. The second thing you should do is not necessarily apologize for what you said or did, but instead commit to never repeating the behavior again.

When you feel angry about something in your past, recall that according to the principle of cause and effect, it was you who originated the cause that led to the effect that incited your anger. Once you adopt this perspective, it is actually quite challenging to get angry at anyone for more than a moment or two. On the contrary, you learn to leave the disempowering victim role behind, and instead look for the deeper meaning or lesson behind each of the difficult situations that you encounter.

Whenever you are reminiscing about the good times in the past, understand that this type of thinking also keeps you from fully experiencing the present moment. Ideally, what you need to learn to do is to completely experience whatever it is you're experiencing at any given time – both good and bad – and then let it go.

In general, anytime you think that it is your past that is driving your future, picture yourself driving a boat, and remember that it is not the wake that is driving the boat. The truth is that your past is not driving your boat (or life) in the present moment, your current thoughts and feelings are. The past can only affect you in the present when you insist on wasting your creative thought and feeling energy on something that exists only in your own mind. Also, adopt the mindset that whatever happened to you helped you to grow, and therefore in some way it served you.

As for the future, virtually all of the thoughts you entertain about it are grounded in fear. The desire to know what is to occur, and the perceived need to make detailed plans to ensure long-term security are both related to the ego's need for safety, resulting from its ardently held fear of death.

The reality is that planning for the future is not nearly as important as keeping your highly creative thought and feeling energies concentrated in the present. To have the outcome you desire, you need to clearly set your intent today, and simply do your best each day to focus on what you do want rather than what you don't want.

When you do let your fears get the upper hand, what you are essentially doing is inadvertently allocating more of your powerful creative thought and feeling energy toward concerns about *not* getting what you want. It can be challenging to leave this behavior behind, primarily because the ego's strong desire for security tends to propel the mind into 'future-thought'. To overcome this, work toward becoming more a conscious *observer* of your thoughts, and then learn to give the minimum amount of energy to those that are related to the future.

Being fully in the present is a skill that requires constant practice, and the key to mastering it is to continually remind yourself to focus on what you are doing or experiencing 'right now'. It is also important to pay greater attention to all of the sensory input that your body is receiving at any given moment. By sharpening your sensory awareness in this way, you will eventually find yourself living more and more fully in the present moment.

Related Reading

Eckhart Tolle, *The Power of Now* (in its entirety)

Richard & Mary-Alice Jafolla, *The Quest, A Journey of Spiritual Rediscovery*: Chapter 29

Fr. Anthony DeMello, *Awareness*: Cultural Conditioning; Clinging to Illusion; Dead Ahead

Dan Millman, *The Laws of Spirit*: The Law of Presence

Neale Donald Walsch, *Conversations with God, Book 1*: Chapter 5

Alan Cohen, *Dare to Be Yourself*: Dare to Live Now

In our next chapter the principle of *Oneness* is discussed.

6: Oneness

I am he,
as you are he,
as you are me,
and we are all together. [65]

THE BEATLES
"I AM THE WALRUS"

The principle of *Oneness* states in effect that, at a fundamental level, literally everything in the Universe is connected to everything else. This is not merely some idealistic spiritual tenet; rather it has been an accepted scientific fact ever since Albert Einstein and other prominent physicists first established that the atom was not creation's lowest common denominator. According to Deepak Chopra:

The material world is full of familiar objects that we
can see, feel, touch, taste and smell. As big objects become
small, shrinking to the size of atoms, our senses fail us.
Theoretically the shrinkage has to stop somewhere,
because no atom is smaller than hydrogen,
the first material particle to be born out of the Big Bang.
But in fact an amazing transformation happens beyond
the atom—everything solid disappears.
Atoms are composed of vibrating energy packets that
have no solidity at all, no mass or size,
nothing for the senses to see or touch.
The Latin word for packet or package is quantum,
the word chosen to describe one unit of energy
inside the atom, and as it turned out,
a new level of reality. [66]

---

[65] John Lennon and Paul McCartney, Copyright © 1967 by Northern Songs Limited/EMI (All rights reserved. Used by permission from Sony ATV Music Publishing.) From the album *Magical Mystery Tour*, (The Gramophone Co. Ltd.,1967).

[66] Deepak Chopra, *How To Know God*, (New York, NY: Harmony Books, 2000) p. 29

It is not my intent here to move into a comprehensive discussion of quantum physics as it relates to spirituality; that subject is thoroughly elaborated upon in the works of highly respected authors such as Deepak Chopra, Gary Zukav, and a number of others. Rather, my point in referencing this information, is to demonstrate that there is hard scientific evidence which unequivocally proves that all things in the Universe are composed of the same basic stuff, namely *energy*.

Essentially what this means is that at the quantum level, you and I are in effect no different than a rock, a tree, empty space, or for that matter anything else in the Universe. More importantly, this raw material of creation does not simply manifest as separate three-dimensional objects, but is, in reality, a *field* of energy that permeates every square inch of the Universe, and as such, connects everything.

As a visual analogy, think of this basic raw material of the Universe as resembling the essence of the *Terminator* character that appeared in one of those very popular movies starring Arnold Schwarzenegger. This pervasive energy field can manifest in countless numbers of ways, creating the illusion of separateness. Yet in actuality, all of its manifestations share the same basic nature, and are in fact linked. Now if that analogy leaves you feeling somewhat uncertain about the nature of this field, consider this additional one from Stuart Wilde:

> *Imagine a large beach ball that's pumped full of air.*
> *Take a few Lego bricks and figures from your kid's toy pile,*
> *and glue them on to the surface of the beach ball.*
> *Now, imagine that you could turn the ball inside out.*
> *The outside of the ball would be smooth, and all the Lego*
> *buildings and people would be stuck to the inside*
> *skin of the ball. A little Lego person living inside the*
> *beach ball would say, "I am over here, and the red Lego building*
> *is over there, so the building is external to me." But in fact,*
> *everything is inside the ball—the building, the air,*
> *the Lego figures, with all their thoughts and feelings.*[67]

---

[67] Stuart Wilde, *Infinite Self*, (Carlsbad, California: Hay House, Inc., 1996) p. 30–31

This is a challenging concept for the human mind to comprehend, as obviously it is much easier to see the separation that exists between us and all other aspects of creation. Therefore, seeing things from the perspective of *Oneness* requires that we accept as true that which we cannot in actuality verify via our senses.

This is a difficult task for most people, yet is worthwhile noting that we human beings have also learned to accept other notions that are not directly verifiable by our senses. For example, we cannot see the infrared signals that are emitted from our television remote controls, but we know that something must be flying through the air or the channels would not change. Another relevant example is cellular phones, as we are now well aware, they enable us to have conversations with people all over the world, but once again we cannot see the actual connection that exists between the phones.

The difference with *Oneness* is that although definitive scientific evidence exists to support it, people automatically tend to default to the perception that each of us is separate from everyone and everything else as well. Yet, when you are willing to make an effort to step aside from that viewpoint, at a minimum you will see some very obvious indications of the connection that exists between human beings. For example, according to Wayne Dyer in his book *Manifest Your Destiny*:

> *Notice that everyone breathes the same air, walks on the*
> *same ground and thinks as an organism, just like you.*
> *You are, indeed, connected to all of these beings.*
> *It is not an accident that someone living in a distant country,*
> *with different outward physical characteristics and separate language,*
> *could die and donate his or her liver or kidney or cornea to you,*
> *and it would accommodate the life force flowing in you.*[68]

---

[68] Wayne W. Dyer, *Manifest Your Destiny*, op. cit., p. 42

SEPARATION IS A CONDITIONED PERCEPTION

As the above passage points out, the evidence of *Oneness* or 'connectedness' between humans is quite convincing. So why is it that the majority of people aren't able to truly sense that connection? The answer is that all of us have been strongly conditioned to see separation instead. Just look around you, and you will see indications of it everywhere you turn, as we literally place labels on everyone that we encounter (e.g., white, black, American, Catholic, conservative, liberal, etc.)

The truth about labels is that they really say nothing about the essence of the person to whom we apply them. They speak only of the 'me' not the 'I', and are merely arbitrary descriptions that serve to keep us from seeing everyone as who they really are — individual "sparks of the Divine" that are, at the most fundamental level, *no different* than us.

What is particularly paradoxical is that of all the labels we humans apply, it is perhaps the 'religion' label that serves to move people away from *Oneness* and toward separation more than any other. It really is astounding to me that the same religions that commonly use terms like the "brotherhood of man" and "children of God" are also quick to remind their members of the superiority of their own dogma.

It is also a historical fact that religious issues have been, and continue to be, at the foundation of both minor and major military conflicts all over the world. For that matter, it has even been estimated that more than one billion people have been killed in wars related to Christianity alone. When you consider the centuries-old religious conflicts in Northern Ireland, the Middle East, the Balkans, and many others, one literally has to be amazed at the irony of it all. All of this can make one appreciate this classic comment from Mahatma Ghandi all the more, "In heaven there is no religion, *thank God*."

EMBRACING ONENESS IN YOUR LIFE

Before you're caught by your own selfishness,
You must confess, we are all in this together.[69]

TODD RUNDGREN
"WHO'S SORRY NOW?"

Embracing the concept of *Oneness* is clearly very challenging because it requires you to step outside of your programming and be willing to look at the world in an entirely new way. Once you have the willingness, it is then a matter of making the daily conscious effort to remind yourself that *yes*; you are indeed connected to everything else in the Universe.

This of course, takes quite of bit of practice, because you literally have to go beyond your senses, since they do not allow you to see or readily feel the energy connecting you to the rest of creation. Therefore, what you need to do is acknowledge this connection actually does exist, just like you came to accept the presence of television and radio waves. As you work to accomplish this, little by little your mindset will change, because as discussed previously in Chapter 3, whatever you focus your thoughts and feelings on will always expand in your consciousness.

Learning to acknowledge your connection to people, in particular, requires that you look very closely at the labels you apply to yourself and to others as well. The truth is that the use of labels is always problematic, because as soon as you apply such a definition to yourself or someone else, you immediately move out of *Oneness* and into separation.

What has worked very well for me, is to internally refer to myself as a 'human being' rather than as an American, or an entrepreneur, or any other particular label. When other people are introduced to me, I politely listen to how they describe themselves, (e.g., nationality

---

[69] Todd Rundgren, Copyright © 1990 by Fiction Music, Inc. adm. By Warner Tamerlane Pub. Corp (BMI) (All rights reserved. Used by permission.) From the CD *Second Wind*, (Warner Bros. Records, Inc., a Time Warner Company. 1990).

and/or profession), acknowledge them as necessary, and then silently remind myself that they are indeed fundamentally just like me.

Additionally, whenever I interact with anyone in any way (e.g., via phone or personal conversation, in passing, in traffic, etc.), I make my best effort to remember that whatever force is beating my heart is beating theirs as well. Finally, whenever I do catch myself labeling someone, I have also developed the practice of immediately sending a silent thought of acceptance to that particular person.

If you were to follow similar approaches, I am confident that you will find it easier and easier to accept the principle of *Oneness*. As you do so, you will discover that most of the discord in your life will tend to disappear, and you will likewise notice yourself having a greater appreciation for all of life.

Speaking from personal experience, it takes time to teach yourself to see the *Oneness* of humanity, as well as everything else; as we discussed earlier, you have been conditioned to look for differences (i.e., separation) from the time you were a child.

In my own case, even though it has been years since I was first exposed to this concept, I still grapple with it each day, simply because it is very easy to backslide into thoughts of separation. To counteract this tendency, I have found that all you can really do is extend your best efforts to at least become more *aware* of when you are seeing separation instead of *Oneness*.

JUDGMENT

No discussion of the principle of *Oneness* would be complete without allocating some time to talk about the concept of judgment. This particular human behavior (i.e., labeling, criticizing, condemning, and so on) plays a significant role in fostering separation. For whatever reason, our minds have what appears to be a natural tendency to pass judgment on people, places, situations, etc.

While no one wants to be considered judgmental, as this description carries a very negative connotation, the fact is that everyone does judge. It is essentially impossible to completely avoid making judgments, for nearly every one of our thoughts has some judgment associated with it.

For example, to describe a meal as delicious is a judgment, as is making a comment that a particular person is attractive. However, it is critical here to make a distinction between the terms judgment and observation. The former involves applying your *opinion* along with *emotion*, while the latter involves merely commenting on what you notice.

In any event, the first step in addressing your tendency to judge is to simply admit to yourself that you do judge. This does not imply by any means that you are a judgmental person; it simply means that you acknowledge this behavioral inclination rather than deny it. As you come to accept that you do regularly judge, you can then begin to become more aware of when you are doing so.

Judging Others

It is also very important to come to an understanding of what the essence of judging other people is really all about. In particular, the reason that we judge others is that we see them, not as *they* are, but as *we* are. In other words, we filter them through *our* belief system. Therefore, our judgments do not really say anything about the other person; they merely describe what our preferences are. Whenever someone doesn't 'match up' to our personal standards, we automatically place some sort of judgment on them.

When I first came to this awareness about judgment, it was a bit of shock to me because, prior to that, I had been a person who constantly criticized other people. In fact, during the time I was working in my first job after graduate school, I was given the nickname 'character assassin' simply because of my proven ability to make fun of other people. Reflecting back upon that time in my life, the fact is that, deep down inside, I *knew* that judging others was wrong, but I had no awareness as to why.

Once I came to understand that judging others simply defined *my* preferences, and that people would go on being whatever they were being despite those preferences, life has never been quite the same for me. Sure, I still have a day-to-day tendency to judge, but the difference is that now I at least have some awareness of when I am moving into judgment, whereas in the past I was oblivious to it. This awareness is not just at an intellectual level, but is often physically based as well, as sometimes I honestly *feel* a sensation in the pit in my stomach when I am being judgmental.

Another very important point to understand about judgment is described in this passage from a very interesting book called, *You Are The Answer*, by Michael J. Tamura:

> *We may fool ourselves into believing that we are*
> *fundamentally different from the person we are judging,*
> *but, in truth, we can never recognize in another*
> *what we don't have in ourselves.*[70]

Please read the above quotation again and take a few moments to ponder it; this can be a very difficult concept to comprehend. What it essentially means is that whatever strongly irritates you about someone else is actually mirroring back to you an aspect of yourself that you have denied, suppressed, or not yet learned to love. This excerpt from Debbie Ford's *The Dark Side of the Light Chasers* builds upon this very important point:

> *Our indignation over the behavior of others is*
> *usually about an unresolved aspect of ourselves.*
> *If we listen to everything that comes out of our mouths*
> *when we talk to others, judge others, or give advice,*
> *we should just turn it around and give it to ourselves.*[71]

This is undoubtedly a challenging concept for us to accept,

---

[70] Michael J. Tamura, *You Are The Answer*, (Parker, CO: Star of Peace Publishing, 2002) p. 125

[71] Debbie Ford, *The Dark Side of the Light Chasers*, (New York, NY: Avon Books, 1998) p. 44–45

particularly because at a conscious level, we are virtually unaware that these aspects even exist. However, if you are open-minded enough to give it some credence, it can provide you with another method for coming to a better understanding of yourself.

Look Within When Judging

For example, when you do find yourself judging, you can use it as an opportunity to look within and ask yourself, "What is it that this person is showing me about myself?" The answer may not come immediately, but if you are sincere in your intent to discover it, eventually you will.

I personally have learned a lot about myself by applying this approach; usually finding what really annoys me about someone else is a behavior that I myself used to engage in. For instance, I now tend to become quite bothered by people who make it a regular practice to criticize other people. Yet, as discussed earlier, at one point I behaved in precisely the same way. If you are truly honest with yourself in this process, it is quite probable that you will likewise make comparable discoveries.

Judgment and Your Connection to Divinity

A final point to be aware of regarding judgment is that participating in it actually serves to interfere with your connection with Divinity itself. Deepak Chopra addresses this point in the following passage from his book *The Seven Spiritual Laws of Success*:

> *When you are constantly evaluating, classifying, labeling,*
> *analyzing, you create a lot of turbulence in your inner dialogue.*
> *This turbulence constricts the flow of energy between you*
> *and the field of pure potentiality. You literally squeeze*
> *the "gap" between thoughts. The gap is your connection to*
> *the field of pure potentiality. It is that state of pure*
> *awareness, that silent space between thoughts, that*
> *inner stillness that connects you to true power.*[72]

---

[72] Deepak Chopra, *The Seven Spiritual Laws of Success*, op. cit., p. 17

This "field of pure potentiality," also known as the 'God Force', is the source of all your creativity. As such, participating in judgment not only fosters separation between you and fellow souls, but also limits your personal power and your overall creative potential as well. It is therefore in your best interest to reduce the amount of judging that you do on a daily basis.

This, of course, takes a lot of practice, but once you come to the awareness that judging does not in any way serve you, it becomes virtually impossible to judge and not feel a bit awkward about doing so. As you do make progress in your effort to move away from judgment, you will not only experience a quieter mind, but will also have a greater feeling of 'connectedness' with all human beings, and with all other elements of creation as well.

As we leave the topic of *Oneness*, I will share with you a powerful passage about this principle that appears in Neale Donald Walsch's best-selling book, *Friendship with God*:

> *For this is the New Gospel: There is no master race.*
> *There is no greatest nation. There is no one true religion.*
> *There is no inherently perfect philosophy. There is no always*
> *right political party, morally supreme economic system, or one and*
> *only way to heaven. Erase these ideas from your memory.*
> *Eliminate them from your experience.*
> *Eradicate them from your culture.*
> *For these are thoughts of division and separation,*
> *and you have killed each other over these thoughts.*
> *Only the truth I give you here will save you: WE ARE ONE.*
> *Carry this message far and wide, across oceans and over continents,*
> *around the corner and around the world.*[73]

So, will *you* now choose to carry this message of *Oneness* forward

---

[73] Neale Donald Walsch, *Friendship with God*, (New York, NY: G.P. Putnam's Sons, 1998) p. 359

in your own life, or will you instead continue to view yourself as separate from everyone and everything else? The freedom to choose is clearly yours.

SUMMING IT ALL UP

The principle of *Oneness* states that, at the basic level, all things in the Universe are connected to all other things. This is not simply a theoretical concept, but has been an acknowledged scientific fact ever since physicists proved that the atom was not the lowest common denominator of all of creation.

The truth is that all things in the Universe are composed of the same basic substance, namely *energy*. Moreover, this energy that is at the foundation of all things is part of a field that permeates every square inch of the Universe, manifesting in countless ways, and with all manifestations intertwined.

Oneness is a challenging concept to accept simply because our senses cannot directly experience it. Yet, we regularly accept other notions that defy our senses, such as wireless phones. The difference with *Oneness* is that, in spite of the scientific evidence that confirms its existence, it appears to be a natural tendency for people to perceive separation instead.

To move beyond this limitation, it is necessary that you at least begin to acknowledge the obvious ways in which human beings are connected. In addition, you need to work to overcome your conditioning, which has taught you to apply labels to literally everyone that you encounter. To move beyond labeling, you must reach the point where you define yourself and everyone else simply as a 'human being'.

Embracing *Oneness* requires that you first make the decision to begin viewing the world in an entirely new way; and second, that you make a conscious effort each day to remind yourself that you are indeed connected to everything else in the Universe. Naturally this takes some practice, because it effectively requires that you ignore what your senses are telling you, and instead simply accept that

Oneness is a valid concept.

Judgment of others plays a significant role in furthering separation. While none of us wants to be considered judgmental, the fact is that all human beings have the tendency to judge. Once you honestly admit to having this inclination, you can then begin to become more conscious about it when you are doing so.

The critical thing to understand about judgment is that when you judge you do not really see people as *they* are, you see them as *you* are. Your judgments only say something about you. Another key point about judgment to remember is that what strongly annoys you about another is in reality an unaccepted aspect of yourself. Once you embrace this concept, you can start to look beyond the surface of your judgments in an attempt to identify what it is that this person you are judging is showing you about yourself.

All of the judging, evaluating, and labeling that you do also serves to create a lot of turmoil in your inner dialogue, and in the process restricts the flow of energy between you and the God-Force. Consequently, judgment not only serves to separate you from your fellow souls, but also tends to reduce your ability to manifest that which you desire.

While adopting the principle of *Oneness* does require regular, daily effort on your part, as you come to embrace it, you will find that the ultimate result will indeed be a more harmonious and rewarding life.

Related Reading

Deepak Chopra, *How To Know God*: Chapter 2

Stuart Wilde, *Infinite Self*: Step 2, Expanding Your Awareness

Wayne W. Dyer, *Manifest Your Destiny*: The Third Principle

Michael J. Tamura, *You Are The Answer*: Chapter 9

Debbie Ford, *The Dark Side of the Light Chasers*: Chapter 4

Deepak Chopra, *The Seven Spiritual Laws of Success*: Chapter 1

Neale Donald Walsch, *Friendship with God*: Chapter Seventeen

In the next chapter the often-misunderstood spiritual principle of *Abundance* is discussed.

7: Abundance

When you sleep on the ground,
With the stars in your face,
You can feel the full length
of the beauty and grace. [74]

DAN FOGELBERG
"THE WILD PLACES"

The principle of *Abundance* is grounded in the concept that the Universe itself is an ever-expanding energy field of unlimited potentiality. Just a glance at our solar system alone reveals the existence of thousands if not millions of stars, yet astronomers agree that what our most powerful telescopes can see represents just a tiny portion of the Universe as a whole. Both astronomers and quantum physicists alike also concur that the Universe as we know it is likewise involved in a constant process of expansion.

ABUNDANCE AS A NATURAL STATE

Just as abundance is the natural state of the entire Universe, so it is for our beloved planet Earth as well. If you merely take a moment to expand your awareness, and truly take *notice* of the incredible abundance that characterizes both the Earth and all the heavens that surround it, you literally cannot help being awed by it all. In that regard, consider this passage from Stuart Wilde:

> *Make a point of noticing the plum tree full of fruit,*
> *gaze at fields of wheat, meditate on the endless rows of*
> *vegetables at the supermarket, and accept the warmth of the*
> *sun as it rises each morning. Also, engage your childlike self,*
> *with awe, in the abundance of stars in the night sky.*
> *Each of these are signposts of the Universe-at-Large reminding*
> *you that you have the gift of life—that your journey*
> *takes place on a planet that is blessed and chock full of*
> *everything that you're ever going to need.* [75]

---

[74] Daniel Fogelberg, Copyright © 1990 by EMI April Music Inc./Hickory Grove Music (ASCAP) (All rights reserved. Used by permission.) From the CD *Wild Places*, (CBS Records and manufactured by Epic Records. 1990).

[75] Stuart Wilde, *The Little Money Bible*, (Carslbad, California: Hay House, Inc., 1998) p. 7

This, of course, runs contrary to the conventional thinking about the Earth's alleged 'limited' resources, but this age-old view misses one very key point — that with the God-Force, there cannot possibly be any limitations. According to Richard and Mary-Alice Jafolla in *The Quest*:

> *The old belief was that there is not enough abundance*
> *to go around, and so we thought if you get yours, I lose mine.*
> *If I get some abundance, I have to deprive you of yours,*
> *I lose mine. We have believed that people are constantly*
> *waiting out there to take our good from us. We thought that*
> *there is only so much substance in this world, and therefore*
> *it can be used up. The human race has had it all wrong.*
> *We have to re-educate ourselves so that we firmly realize*
> *that God's source of good is unlimited. God, by nature,*
> *is a creative process, always capable of, (and desirous of)*
> *bringing new and more into our lives.*[76]

The Truth of Abundance

So there is indeed always enough for each of us, and there will invariably be ample resources on this planet too, simply because with God all things are possible. For example, while it is undeniable that only so much oil can be extracted from the Earth, it is also true that as extensions of the mind of God, human beings have the unlimited potential to uncover alternative energy sources, as well as to devise new, more efficient ways of using the oil and other fuels that are still available. The same goes for any other of the Earth's so-called 'scarce' resources.

Most people find it challenging to accept this principle, because based on all of the poverty and alleged shortages that exist in the world; it truly 'appears' that scarcity is our natural state. As everyone knows however, appearances can be very deceiving, for what lies

---

[76] Richard and Mary-Alice Jafolla, *The Quest, A Journey of Spiritual Rediscovery,* op. cit., p. 335

behind all of the supposed insufficiency in the world is actually a *scarcity consciousness* that is both shared and promoted by a preponderance of people in the world.

Abundance, Money, and Conditioning

If you doubt this, reflect for a moment on your own thoughts regarding abundance; money in particular. Provided you are like most people, regardless of how much money you may have, you still have concerns about your financial future, and these concerns are primarily based upon your *conditioning* not necessarily on your own personal experience. By conditioning, I mean the beliefs that were handed down to you by your parents or other relatives, along with the programming that you were exposed to by the culture at large.

Let's take a closer look at some of the most common beliefs that many of us received from both our well-meaning relatives and our society/culture:

- *"You better get yours before someone gets theirs, because there is only so much to go around."*
- *"Money is the root of all evil."*
- *"You must struggle to make a living in our competitive world."*
- *"Rich people will find it very difficult to enter the gates of heaven."*

The above list could obviously be expanded, but my intent here is merely to provide some fitting examples of the negative ideas regarding abundance (and money), to which people are commonly exposed. When you pause to consider just how widespread these ideas and beliefs actually are, it really is not surprising that a consciousness of lack becomes prevalent for the vast majority of the population.

If you question that these collectively held beliefs are at the foundation of much of the poverty in the industrialized world, page back to Chapter 3 and read the section titled *"Thoughts are the Currency of Creation."* As discussed elsewhere in this book, whatever we focus on (or believe with feeling) expands in our individual consciousness, and if millions of people think and *feel* that scarcity is the natural state of the Universe, then that becomes, in effect, *their* reality, regardless of evidence to the contrary.

What is really unfortunate, as this next passage from Dr. Wayne Dyer illustrates, is that people are simply unaware that at some level that they themselves are responsible for whatever lack they are experiencing in their lives:

> *If we dwell on scarcity, we are putting energy into what we do not have, and this continues to be our experience of life. The theme of so many people's life story is "I simply do not have enough," or "How can I believe in abundance when my children don't have all the clothes that they need?" or "I would be a lot happier if I had _____." People believe they live a life of lack because they are unlucky, instead of recognizing that their belief system is rooted in scarcity thinking.*[77]

It really is a very basic principle — as an extension of the mind of God (see Chapter 3: Who Are You?) you have enormous creative power, and as such you need to be very careful about what it is you choose to believe. So, if you are not experiencing all of the abundance you desire in your life, recognize this moment that somewhere along the line you adopted beliefs that have caused you to literally push it away from yourself. Once you come to acknowledge this fact, you can then move forward to carefully examine exactly what you have accepted as *your* truth about abundance. From there you can proceed to systematically refute, and then eventually drop any beliefs that are rooted in scarcity.

From my own experience, this process can be a challenging one primarily because our beliefs about abundance, and money in particular, tend to be very deeply embedded within our subconscious minds.

---

[77] Dr. Wayne W. Dyer, *You'll See It When You Believe It*, (New York, NY: William Morrow and Company, 1989) p. 123

In my case, because I was raised by an incredibly frugal father and a mother who always appeared to be concerned about money, it has been a formidable task for me to leave behind some aspects of the conditioning they provided. Even as I write this chapter, I still continue to grapple with some old money issues on a day-to-day basis.

What I have found to be valuable however, is maintaining an attitude of compassion and patience with myself as I continue to progress through the process of healing these longstanding abundance issues. During the past ten years, there have been times when I have made excellent progress, while at other times it almost appeared as if I were going backwards.

The good news to report is that spiritual growth principles have been invaluable to me in my efforts to leave behind non-empowering beliefs regarding abundance, and I am very confident that you can benefit from them as well. In particular, I have made it a practice to apply four suggestions made by many authors of books related to personal and spiritual growth, and have been highly satisfied with the results. All four of these suggestions, as well as my own experiences in applying them, are discussed in the next several pages.

GRATITUDE

The first of these suggestions: to be *grateful* for what we already have in our lives, is a common theme across many spiritual growth books. When you stop and think about it, the fact is that the vast majority of us have much for which to be thankful – we just tend to be oblivious to it.

For example, as mentioned in Chapter 3, most people never give a second thought to the myriad of activities that are occurring within their bodies every second they are alive. Additionally, those of us living in first-world countries rarely, if ever, feel grateful for such things as electricity, indoor plumbing, relatively safe drinking water, and much, much more. Instead, most of us tend to focus on what is missing in our lives, and ignore all of the blessings we already have. In the United States especially, people take so much for granted.

This is truly amazing; in view of the fact that even our nation's poorest people have a higher standard of living than most of the population in developing countries.

Expressing Gratitude to Attract Greater Abundance

As you begin to acknowledge your gratitude for what you already have, you actually open up the door for even greater abundance to come into your life. Since I was exposed to this concept personally, it has been my daily practice to make my best efforts to be grateful for everything that I have or experience in my life.

Each day upon waking, I have developed the habit of saying prayers of gratitude, and throughout the day, I likewise do my best to remember to be grateful for any number of things. For example, when I arrive at a solution to a challenging problem, or experience a thought that provides a timely insight, or even see a flock of geese fly by in full formation, I close my eyes for a second or two and silently (and sometimes *verbally*) express my gratitude for it.

Moreover, each time I receive a check in the mail from one of my clients, I make sure to say thank you for the arrival of that payment. At the end of each day, just as I'm dozing off to sleep, I also make certain to say a prayer of gratitude for everything that I experienced that day (both good and bad), and for the greatest gift of all, *life itself!*

For every moment of joy
Every hour of fear
For every winding road that brought me here
For every breath, for every day of living
This is my Thanksgiving.[78]

DON HENLEY
"MY THANKSGIVING"

---

[78] Don Henley/Stan Lynch/Jai Winding, Copyright © 2000 Wisteria Music BMI/WB Music Corp./Matanzas Music/Dobbs Music (ASCAP) (All rights reserved. Used by permission.) From the CD *Inside Job*, (Warner Bros. Records, Inc., a Time Warner Company. 2000).

Once I adopted an *attitude of gratitude,* much like Mr. Henley describes, I can genuinely say that things began to flow to me more easily than at any other time in my life. It was almost as if the Universe sensed the sincerity of my appreciation, and in exchange began to give me even more for which to be grateful.

The reason that we do experience even greater abundance as a result of expressing heartfelt gratitude, connects back to a fundamental principle we discussed in Chapter 3: Whatever we focus on expands in our consciousness.

If you are not oriented toward gratitude, and are instead concentrating your powerful thought and feeling energies on the scarcity in your life, then just what do you think you will be attracting into your life? The answer unfortunately, is more scarcity. So, start right now to genuinely express gratitude on a daily basis, and over time I believe you will indeed experience greater abundance in your life.

Giving

A second valuable suggestion regarding abundance, as this next quotation illustrates, is related to the importance of giving:

> *The key to prosperity is the realization that prosperity*
> *doesn't come by getting more. It comes by giving more.*
> *The law of prosperity is actually 180 degrees from what*
> *most of us have been taught. We prosper not by concentrating*
> *on what we are getting but by emphasizing what we are giving.*
> *There is simply no way to circumvent this law,*
> *and it may take a quantum shift in your thinking*
> *to bring yourself around to the truth.*[79]

If you are like most people, you have probably heard something very similar on more than one occasion, namely the old cliché "as

---

[79] Richard and Mary-Alice Jafolla, *The Quest, A Journey of Spiritual Rediscovery,* op. cit., p. 335

you give, so shall you receive." This familiar adage has traditionally been interpreted along religious rather than purely spiritual lines. It was commonly thought that an individual who was more giving in nature would in turn receive greater favor from God. While on the surface this may appear to be the case, the truth is the God-Force is not really sitting up there keeping score of your giving practices. Instead, the relationship between giving and receiving ties back to the principles of *Cause and Effect* and *Oneness* that were discussed in previous chapters.

The Principle of "Cause & Effect" and Giving

Remember that every cause you initiate leads to an effect. So, when you give from the heart, you set energy into motion that must in turn find its way back to you in some form. I say in *some* form, because there is no telling how or when the effect may show up.

For example, let's say you donate a sum of money to a cause that has inspired you in some way; this does not necessarily mean that you will receive the same amount or more in return. The positive energy you extended may instead come back to you as a new business or career opportunity that appears seemingly out of nowhere, or it may manifest for you as improved or continued good health, or as a breakthrough in a troubled relationship, etc.

Now you might say that this is not always true, as there are many instances in which people give but do not seem to receive anything positive in return. In some cases this may *appear* to be an accurate appraisal. However, more often than not, if you were able to look deeper into the motivation behind the giving, you would probably discover that their *intent* wasn't quite as pure as one may have originally thought.

Specifically, when the giving is done with the objective of receiving something in return, or because the person feels like they have no other choice but to give, then the underlying motivation behind it is rooted in scarcity. Since the Universe always knows what our real intentions are (i.e., our true *feelings*), it is not surprising then that people who give from this frame of mind do not receive anything in return.

The Principle of "Oneness" and Giving

The principle of *Oneness* relates to 'giving' in a very fundamental way. Namely, that if we are all part of the same unified field of energy, then by definition, anything that we give to another in a heartfelt way, we effectively give to ourselves as well. In that regard, consider this passage from Arnold Patent:

> *There is a principle underlying the concept of giving*
> *and receiving which further encourages giving freely to others.*
> *The principle is that we only give to ourselves. . . .*
> *Giving energy to another person*
> *does not deplete our own supply.*[80]

This concept can take some time to embrace, as your senses are only capable of perceiving a world of matter instead of the pure creative energy of which that matter is composed. When you give something away of a material nature, you immediately conclude that you have lost something, for the basic reason that you are no longer are in possession of it. At the level of pure energy however, what you have done was to conduct an *energy transaction* with the field of pure potentiality. In other words, you have *sown* something into an energy field of which you are a part, so you must likewise *reap* something in return.

Giving from Obligation

Prior to discovering the spiritual path more than a decade ago, virtually the only time I ever donated money was to the Catholic Church as part of the parish's regular tithing program. In truth, I

---

[80] Arnold Patent, *You Can Have It All*, op. cit., p. 65–66

never really understood why I was doing it other than that it was part of my duty as a parishioner. The problem with giving under those circumstances was that the energy of it was not really positive; the primary motivation behind it was one of obligation rather than a heartfelt gesture. In a sense, I participated in this behavior because it was easier than dealing with the guilty feelings that would arise from not supporting the church.

As I evolved in my spiritual growth however, I came to a different understanding about the concepts of giving and/or tithing. I was very strongly affected by the words of Fr. Anthony DeMello, when he commented on his *Wake Up to Life* tape series, "that just about the worst kind of gift you can give is one that is given so that *you don't have a bad feeling.*"

When I first heard this, it was as if a proverbial light went off in my head, simply because it made so much sense to me. How can giving be a positive experience when the underlying motivation for it is a feeling of obligation or guilt? Obviously, it cannot, yet in our world it is very common for people to give solely from that motive.

With that new awareness in place, I established two new standards for donating money to charitable institutions. First, I would no longer give in response to a feeling of obligation. Second, I would only give to causes that applied no less than 90 percent of their total receipts to actually providing services to the intended recipients. With these standards in mind, I then made a commitment to work towards overcoming my longstanding scarcity mentality, by disciplining myself to consistently allocate a portion of my income to causes that met the latter standard.

As a self-employed person, with income that always varies, at first it was a bit of an adjustment to donate money during the leaner times. Early on in the process however, I heard a speech by Dr. Wayne Dyer in which he said that if a person could not bring themselves to give when they had little, then they would never be able to give even when they had a lot. So, no matter how little I earned in a given month, each time I received a payment from a client, it became common practice for me to earmark part of those funds toward donation to selected charities.

In addition, I carried this abundant attitude into other areas of life, as I made it a practice to become more generous in meritorious tipping, and also adopted a different perspective about cash donations, by learning to follow my first instinct rather than my second. Specifically, in the past when someone who was collecting for a specific cause approached me in public, I would ignore my first instinct, which was usually to give paper currency, and instead I'd reach in my pocket to see if there was some loose change available.

Now, if it *feels* right to donate, I just go ahead and give the dollar or two in paper currency that is in my pocket, rather than digging around for coins. When we choose to follow this initial instinct instead of our fear-based intellect, what we are effectively doing is demonstrating to the Universe (i.e., the God-Force) and our subconscious minds, that we have confidence in the universal principle of abundance.

Before leaving the subject of *giving*, I also feel it is important to acknowledge that giving really shouldn't be done for the express purpose of reducing one's taxable income. When you give *just* to qualify for a tax deduction, it is obvious that the energy behind that giving is rooted in scarcity thinking, since you are clearly looking to get something for yourself as well.

On the other hand, if you happen to truly believe in a cause, and it provides you with a tax benefit as well, then of course, that is wonderful. In a similar vein, the fact that making a gift to a particular cause would not be considered tax-deductible should by no means preclude you from donating, if you *feel* like it is the right thing to do.

SPENDING

The third suggestion related to the principle of abundance is to recognize the importance of *spending* money. Deepak Chopra emphasizes this point very clearly in this passage from his best-selling book, *Creating Affluence*:

> *Money is like blood, it must flow. Hoarding and holding*
> *on to it causes sludging. In order to grow, it must flow.*
> *Otherwise it gets blocked and like clotted blood,*
> *it can only cause damage. Money is life energy that we exchange*
> *and use as a result of the service we provide to the Universe.*
> *And in order to keep it coming to us,*
> *we must keep it circulating.*[81]

The concept of money itself will be discussed in some detail later in this chapter, but for our purposes here, I would first like to elaborate a bit on the above quotation. It should *not* be construed to mean that one should spend money indiscriminately by racking up credit card bills and/or exhausting savings accounts. Rather, I believe what Dr. Chopra is essentially saying, is that it is necessary for us to learn to spend money in day-to-day life, without a nagging fear about having enough of it in the future.

Acting Abundantly

Whether it's something as simple as ordering a more expensive entrée at a restaurant, or perhaps buying the optional air conditioning on a new car, by spending money when you *feel* like doing so, you are once again sending a message to the Universe that you are confident that there will always be enough for you. It is much like what was discussed in the previous section about giving, only this time it applies to what you give to *yourself*. To be clear, it is *not* about going into debt by over-spending, but rather putting aside the fear of the future and purchasing some things (i.e., goods, travel, services, etc.) that will bring you some joy or satisfaction in the *present moment*.

---

[81] Deepak Chopra, *Creating Affluence*, op. cit., p. 49; Excerpted from *Creating Affluence* by Deepak Chopra © 1993. Used with permission from New World Library, Novato, CA 94949, www.newworldlibrary.com

Soon after reading *Creating Affluence* back in 1993, I began to put Dr. Chopra's advice into practice as a matter of course. It was demanding at first, as the scarcity programs that were circling around in my head were very deeply embedded, but over time I found it less difficult to spend money without experiencing the same level of anxiety as I had in the past. Interestingly, once I adopted this practice, along with regularly expressing gratitude and giving of myself financially, there has always been more than enough new business revenue for me to offset whatever cash outflows occur.

This is not to imply that by taking up these practices, you will never again experience any issues regarding abundance, because even as I write this I consistently do. The point is that by taking steps, even small ones, we demonstrate that confidence referenced above, and in the process, open the door for even more abundance to arrive.

In order to make this point even stronger, I will now share with you a personal story about a time back in the summer of 2000, when I chose to really put this 'spending' concept to the test. At that time, I made the decision to follow my heart and invest in a dream I had; to spend an entire summer on a Greek island called Alonnisos. My wife and I originally visited there in 1997, at the invitation of her mom and stepfather. They have had a vacation home there since the early 1980s. We returned to Alonnisos again in 1998, and it was during that trip that the inspiration to spend an extended amount of time on the island initially occurred to me.

Throughout the balance of that year and beyond, the same idea just kept popping into my mind, and then one day in June of 1999, a very heartfelt discussion with a friend of mine motivated me to drop the fear and proceed forward. Pursuing this dream however, would require a rather substantial financial commitment, as obviously it would be necessary for us to pay for housing and living expenses in both Greece and back at home as well. Thankfully, my wife agreed to support this dream, and during the fall of 1999 we began making our plans to spend four months in Greece the following summer.

We left during the latter part of May 2000, and returned in late September, with the total cost of the trip being several thousand dollars. Fortunately, with the support of the God-Force and my own hard work, I had earned enough in the months prior to departure to pay for nearly forty percent of it, but that still meant we had to withdraw a rather sizable amount of money from our savings account. This was by no means a small sum to us, as it wouldn't be to most people.

Leaving the U.S. for a four-month period also meant that neither of us would be earning any income, and for me in particular it would require that I put my six year-old freelance writing business on hold. The risk was obvious: my clients would go elsewhere to fulfill their needs, and perhaps by the time I returned home there might no longer be any customers to serve.

Interestingly, (and this is the key point of the story) within five days after returning from the trip I was contacted by three of my clients. By the time eleven weeks had elapsed, I was able to earn *more than two times* the amount of money we had removed from our savings account. To say I felt incredibly blessed by all of this would be an understatement, but the truth is that throughout the entire trip, I never once doubted that things would work out one way or another.

It is now very clear to me that my willingness to invest in this dream did in fact demonstrate to the Universe that I truly felt confident about my financial future, and the result was that even more abundance flowed to me upon my return. This, combined with the fact that the four-month sabbatical allowed me to write more than four chapters of this book, made the trip a complete success.

While perhaps you are not currently in a position to take off and leave the country for four months, the moral of the story is still the same. When you make the decision to invest in anything that you *feel* strongly about having or doing, no matter how inexpensive or costly, you are showing your faith that the Universe will in turn provide you with opportunities to experience even greater abundance.

DOING WHAT YOU LOVE

Someplace inside you
A river is waiting to flow,
Will you let it go?[82]

DAN FOGELBERG
"MAN IN THE MIRROR"

The fourth suggestion I'd like to share with you regarding abundance—the importance of *doing what you love*—is one that is
embraced by virtually all of this era's most prominent personal and
spiritual growth authors. The adage "do what you love and the
money will follow" is very commonly known, but just why is this so?
In response to this question, reflect upon the following passage from
Arnold Patent:

When you choose to make doing what you love the core
experience of your life, you move into alignment with the Universe.
Immediately, the infinite supply of energy is available to you.
You feel the aliveness that comes from having the unlimited
energy of the Universe flow through you.
This aliveness influences the energy signals you emit,
and the people and circumstances that will support the continuation
of your feeling of aliveness are attracted to you.[83]

Effortless Accomplishment

Stop for a moment and think about something that you really love
to do. Now get in touch with the feelings that you normally experience while doing this activity. Assuming you were able to identify
such a pursuit, it is likely that you would typically experience at least
three distinct feelings—a feeling of joy or bliss, a feeling of being in

---

[82] Dan Fogelberg, Copyright © 1975 by Hickory Grove Music (ASCAP) (All rights
reserved. Used by permission.) From the album *Captured Angel*, (CBS Records and
manufactured by Epic Records/CBS Inc. 1975).

[83] Arnold Patent, *You Can Have It All*, op. cit., p. 49–50

the flow, (a.k.a. *effortless accomplishment*), and a feeling of time literally standing still as you instinctively stay focused in the present
moment. As the preceding passage from Mr. Patent infers, these
feelings arise because you are effectively tapping into the energy of
your Higher Self, or to put it another way, you are allowing the limitless 'I' to express itself instead of the fearful, self-conscious 'me'.

These times are very magical, because they give you an opportunity to step outside of your active conscious mind and truly become a
channel for the Divine. It really is an exhilarating feeling, because
you are not really thinking about what you're doing, but rather you
are *feeling* it. In my case, I always experience such sensations whenever I am presented with the chance to deliver a presentation to a
live audience. There is nothing else in the world that I love doing
more. It really is an amazing experience, as the words flow from me
without any overt conscious effort on my part. By the time it's all
over, I am actually hard pressed to explain the origin of the information that I shared.

The reality is that you, as well as every other person in the world,
have unique, innate skills that crave to be expressed. While you may
doubt this to be true, remember that the God-Force literally threw
away the blueprint when you were created, so there is no one in this
entire world who can express themselves in exactly the same way.
Others might argue that there was no way that anyone would pay
them for doing what they love, or that there aren't enough opportunities available in their area of interest. In response to that, consider
this next quotation from Dr. Wayne Dyer:

> *There is no scarcity of opportunity to make a living*
> *at what you love, there is only scarcity of resolve*
> *to make it happen. Whatever you love doing more*
> *than anything else has built within it an opportunity*
> *to make a living at it, even though you may not believe it.*
> *Your fears of doing what you truly love are based on a belief*
> *that you are going to go broke and be unable to pay your bills*

and meet your family responsibilities. Not so! . . .
If you have always paid your bills, why would you suddenly
become the kind of person who does not?[84]

As mentioned earlier, once you do make the decision to do what you love to do, you move into right alignment with the Universe. This in turn, opens the door for all kinds of new energies and opportunities to migrate towards you. The reason is simple, as you do what you love, you emit a positive energy that will attract the necessary people and circumstances to assist you on your path. As for concerns about meeting your financial obligations, Dyer is right. If you have always been a responsible person, why all of a sudden would you become irresponsible? I have certainly found this to be true. Once I made the commitment to doing the work I love (i.e., inspirational writing and speaking), seemingly out of nowhere people began to show up to help me, and opportunities to earn money arrived unexpectedly as well.

The Risk of Not Doing What You Love

If you are still unconvinced regarding this concept of doing what you love, then take a closer look at just what you are accomplishing by spending your time doing work you dislike, just to pay the bills. By remaining in this type of situation, what you are effectively doing is focusing your powerful thought and feeling energy on something that you clearly don't like, and the ultimate result will be your attraction of more of the same. On the contrary, if you use that energy to vividly picture yourself spending time doing what you really love – and remain focused on that picture – you very well might find yourself doing it one day.

Putting Love Into Your Existing Work

If you are a person that simply cannot envision yourself feeling comfortable about leaving a so-called secure position to do what you

---

[84] Dr. Wayne W. Dyer, *You'll See It When You Believe It*, op. cit., p. 147

love, then it is truly critical for you to develop a different attitude regarding your existing employment. For example, consider using the following affirmation each day prior to heading off to work: "*I do what I love, and I love what I do.*"

When I initially heard this recommendation during a live presentation given by Dr. Wayne Dyer, it sounded a bit too simplistic to me, but based on my own experience in applying it over time, I can genuinely say that when it is used with an open mind, it can really help to improve the circumstances of one's existing employment.

In my case, I used that affirmation to reframe my work as a freelance technical writer, by recognizing that this work not only provided me with the opportunity to earn a reasonable income, but also gave me a forum to practice being 'inspirational' (when appropriate) to any individual whose path I came across. In a sense, what I set my intent to do was to put as much love into my work as possible, and to address each project with an attitude of service, as well as true compassion for the person for whom I was writing. Additionally, I made a point to always express gratitude for whatever work 'showed up', for that assignment was a blessing that assisted me in meeting my financial obligations.

Interestingly, soon after I put this approach into practice two things occurred. First, my business began to grow, and second, the work itself became somewhat more enjoyable for me. Now, if you apply a similar approach to your current work, there is no guarantee that you will experience the same results, but I am confident that you will, at a minimum, notice an improvement in your work environment, simply because you've chosen to bring a more positive energy to the situation. From there, who knows what could happen? You just may wind up attracting someone into your life who can assist you in moving into more satisfying work.

MONEY

Any discussion regarding the principle of abundance would be incomplete without spending some time in addressing the subject of *money*, though my purpose here is not to provide a complete discourse on the topic. There are scores of books that focus on doing exactly that. Instead, my intention is to clearly define what money is, as well as what it is not, and also to clear up some of the common misconceptions that people have regarding it.

As stated earlier in the section on *spending*, money is simply a medium of exchange, and yet if you queried the average person, many would choose to define money as abundance itself. The fact is however, that abundance is much more than money alone. Abundance is the pure potentiality of the God-Force itself, the gift of life and of nature with all of its diversity and splendor, the blessings of perfect health and satisfying relationships, the joyful feeling associated with having a purpose in life.

This and even more is what abundance is really all about, and while money plays a part in it, it is by no means the symbol of abundance. There are – no doubt – millions of people who have significant sums of money, and still perceive themselves as lacking in one way or another. This is not to suggest that money is not important, for in modern society it certainly is. What *is* necessary for you to learn, however is to keep money in perspective by recognizing it as simply one aspect of what comprises an abundant life.

Limiting Beliefs About Money

Besides putting money in the proper perspective, you also need to complete an inventory of just what it is that you do believe about money. Strangely enough, while money is one of the most talked about and sought after commodities in the world, the truth is that the majority of us have been taught some very negative things about money. As mentioned earlier in this chapter, it is very common to hear phrases such as, "money is the root of all evil" and "filthy rich," not only as we are growing up but into adulthood as well.

While beliefs of this nature do not serve anyone in any way, people often find them hard to leave behind completely, primarily because they were learned very early in life. If you are a person that still carries even remnants of such beliefs, what you need to do first is identify them, then begin to systematically dispute them, and finally, make your best efforts to replace them with those of a more empowering nature.

In my experience, an effective technique that can be used for disputing unwanted beliefs is based on a type of psychotherapy espoused by the Institute for Rational-Emotive Therapy (RET) based in New York. As a matter of background, I was originally introduced to RET during the latter part of 1990, and over time had great success in applying it towards some very limiting beliefs I carried regarding both love relationships and money.

RET recommends the technique of applying a scientific method by using reason, logic and facts to counter 'irrational' beliefs. For example, once you identify a limiting belief, you first write it down on a piece of paper, and then below that write down the following questions:

- *Is this belief realistic and factual?*
- *Is this belief logical?*
- *Is this belief flexible and non-rigid?*
- *Can this belief be falsified?*
- *Does this belief ensure that I will get good, happy results by continuing to hold it?*

The next step is to respond to those questions using a thoughtful, rational approach. For instance, let's say that the unwanted or irrational belief that we want to challenge is "money is the root of all evil." In response to question one, we could say this belief is not realistic because it is far too general in nature, and it is by no means factual because we could identify a number of so-called evil things, events, or people that have no relationship to money.

For example, consider a person that verbally abuses a spouse about his or her physical appearance. That could certainly qualify as 'evil' behavior, yet it's difficult, at best, to demonstrate any direct correlation existing between money itself and the acting out of such behavior. Or, if money is truly at the root of all evil in the world, then how do you explain all of the good that charitable organizations accomplish with the donations they receive?

I could go on with more arguments to dispute this belief, but I will make the assumption at this point that you have gotten a good feel for how RET works from a conceptual point of view. Naturally, you would apply this same approach in answering the other questions.

The act itself – writing down arguments to dispute unwanted and/or limiting beliefs – sends a strong message of reprogramming to your subconscious mind. To further reinforce that message, you can also record your responses on tape with *feeling*, and then listen to them in your car or on a cassette player as you are going to sleep at night. Repetition is critical, since it clearly played a pivotal role in anchoring the limiting beliefs into your consciousness in the first place.

This is just one of several techniques for disputing irrational beliefs that are available within RET. For complete details regarding this very practical approach to psychotherapy, check out either of these two books by the founder of RET, Dr. Albert Ellis: *A New Guide to Rational Living*, or *How to Stubbornly Refuse to Make Yourself Miserable About Anything*.

Adopting More Empowering Money Beliefs

As you move through the process of liberating yourself from the limiting beliefs you have about money, you will of course need to replace them with new, more empowering ones. Obviously it is up to you to identify exactly what beliefs to embrace, but I do have some general suggestions for you. First, there is absolutely nothing wrong with adopting a belief like, "I love money, and money loves me" or something similar. As long as you are clear that at the most fundamental level, what you really love is the additional *freedom* that will emerge when you open up to allow more money to flow into your life.

Second, to assist you in building your new inventory of beliefs about money, take the time to read a selection of spiritual growth books that have a focus on money and/or abundance. There are a number of such works available at most major, full-line bookstores. I personally recommend two books by Stuart Wilde: *The Little Money Bible*, and *The Trick to Money is Having Some*.

Another excellent book in this category is *Abundance and Right Livelihood,* which is the text of a stimulating workshop conducted by *Conversations with God* author Neale Donald Walsch. As you invest the time to peruse the bookstore, you may, of course, uncover other titles that appeal to you even more.

Third, make it a practice to write and then regularly use affirmations that reinforce the new beliefs you are seeking to hardwire into your consciousness, so to speak. As mentioned in Chapter 2, affirmations can be very valuable tools for conscious change, providing, of course, that you have acquired a clear understanding of how best to use them. In this regard, I highly recommend an informative 'how-to' book on this subject by Stuart Wilde that is quite simply called, *Affirmations*.

Soon after reading that book in 1997, I initiated a regular ritual of saying affirmations as part of my own spiritual practice (e.g., "I always have more money coming into my household than going out."), and that ritual continues to this day. Over this timeframe, I have discovered that affirmations truly do work, but their value is not always quickly discernible, as it can take some time for the effort to fully bear fruit. In addition, at times the result that ultimately manifests isn't exactly what we originally envisioned, but nonetheless provides the essence of what we desired. Finally, I have also noticed that the effects of applying them tend to emerge in a very gradual and somewhat subtle fashion. So the key is to simply stay with the practice and remain patient, for as an old saying goes, *infinite patience produces immediate results.*

My fourth and final suggestion is that whatever new beliefs about money you choose to embrace, seek to remember that from your soul's perspective, the overriding purpose for having money is to use it to buy 'life experiences'.

> *You spend your whole life*
> *just pilin' it up there,*
> *You've got stacks and stacks and stacks*
> *Then, Gabriel comes and taps you on the shoulder,*
> *But you don't see no hearses with luggage racks.*[85]
>
> DON HENLEY
> "GIMME WHAT YOU GOT"

As the above song lyric clearly indicates, whenever you do depart this earth, neither your money nor any of your possessions will go with you. Interestingly though, while most all of us are intellectually aware of this, many people throughout the world, and particularly in Western society, remain intent upon accumulating as much money and stuff as they possibly can. This is not to suggest that there is anything wrong with spending money, for as we learned earlier in this chapter, the act of spending itself can serve to demonstrate confidence in our abundance.

The problem that arises when accumulation itself is the goal is that not only do we become inordinately focused on collecting money and material goods, but we then also take it a step further by putting an enormous amount of energy into doing whatever is necessary to *hold on* to what we have. When you compare this typical 'adult' behavior to how we behaved as very young children, you can see that we have virtually lost the ability to truly enjoy something for its very essence — the *experience* or *feeling* it provides us.

If you doubt this to be true, just take a few moments to observe a very young child (i.e., one to two years old) at play in a playpen full

---

[85] Don Henley, Stan Lynch and John Corey, Copyright © 1988 Cass County Music/Matanzas Music (ASCAP) (All rights reserved. Used by permission.) From the CD *The End of the Innocence*, (The David Geffen Company, manufactured exclusively by Warner Bros. Records, Inc., a Time Warner Company. 1988).

of toys. Unlike adults, that child will fully experience the toy, and then typically move on to the next toy without a concern about what happens to the first toy. This is because part of a child's natural instinct is to experience as much of life as he or she can, and also to remain unattached to things. However, as that child grows up he or she learns from so-called 'wise' adults, as well as some of his or her own worldly experiences, that it's not really the feeling that is important, but rather that possession of the item itself matters more.

Money Buys 'Experiences'

As this excerpt from Stuart Wilde's book *Infinite Self* emphasizes, as souls inhabiting bodies (and not the other way around), it is indeed essential that we come to the realization that the value in money derives from the 'experiences' it allows us to purchase:

> *The whole function of money is not to have it;*
> *its function is to use it. The main reason for generating money*
> *is to buy experiences. You want to get to the end of your life with zilch*
> *in the bank, and look back and say, "My God, look at this*
> *huge pile of experiences," because none of your memories are ever lost.*
> *Everything you've done is in your eternal memory somewhere.*[86]

Once we adopt this attitude about money, what we effectively do is put ourselves in a position to add valuable *experiential mileage* to our souls. While some might contend that you can always pick up any missed experiences in some future lifetime, consider this very simple and obvious truth: *you will never again be the personality you are now.* As such, you should make every effort to live your life to the fullest, and experience all that you possibly can during this incarnation.

It was this concept of buying experiences that played a key role in the decision to invest in our four-month trip to Greece, described earlier in this chapter. Now, nearly three years after our return, I can

---

[86] Stuart Wilde, *Infinite Self*, (Carlsbad, California: Hay House, Inc., 1996) p. 129–130

say with complete confidence that it was one of the best investments I have ever made. It provided us with the opportunity to experience a totally different world than we had ever known. Based on the success of that trip, we have already discussed other travel adventures we would like to experience, and intend to follow through on those as well.

As mentioned earlier, obviously not everyone is in a position to take a four-month sabbatical to Europe or elsewhere. However, it is not necessary to spend thousands of dollars to purchase an experience. For example, you could do something as simple as going to a local spa for your first massage, or perhaps have dinner at the most exclusive restaurant in town. You could also take a course in something like scuba diving, or maybe even skydiving. There are numerous other examples that could be listed here, but the key point is that it is important to use money to experience as much of life as you can, and not primarily for acquiring material goods.

As we conclude this discussion about the principle of abundance, I will leave you with one of my favorite passages regarding this subject that appears in Stuart Wilde's *The Little Money Bible*:

> *It isn't hard to see the abundance of our planet.*
> *You only have to look at the fruit trees in the fall,*
> *the lushness of life. We know that money is not rare*
> *and that abundance is natural. Buckminster Fuller calculated*
> *that if all the wealth of the world was divided equally*
> *among its citizens, each and every one of us would be a millionaire.*
> *It's natural, therefore, for everybody to be*
> *abundant—our natural state is "rich."*[87]

Your natural state is indeed one of abundance, so if you are not currently experiencing all of the abundance that you desire, recognize that having it requires you to first be *willing* to accept that it is always available; second, that you must take undertake some

---

[87] Stuart Wilde, *The Little Money Bible*, op. cit., p. 2

effort to tap into it; and third, that you must truly be open to receive it.

SUMMING IT ALL UP

The principle of *abundance* is based on the premise that the Universe itself is a continually expanding energy field of limitless potentiality. Just as abundance is the natural state of the aggregate Universe, so it is for the Earth as well.

While this runs contrary to the images of poverty and alleged shortages in the world, behind all of this supposed scarcity is a collective consciousness of lack shared by the majority of people. Underlying this consciousness is an assortment of negative beliefs handed down over generations by our parents, relatives and the culture at large.

What is really unfortunate is that people tend to accept such beliefs without question. In doing so, they unknowingly use their innate creative power as extensions of the mind of God to actually create scarcity in their lives via behaviors based on those beliefs. Once you come to understand this, you can then move forward to refute your scarcity-based beliefs and replace them with those of an abundant nature.

The application of spiritual growth principles can definitely assist you in this process of leaving behind non-empowering beliefs regarding abundance. Within this chapter in particular we discussed four valuable suggestions made by a number of prominent authors of personal growth works. The first of these suggestions is to be *grateful* for what you already have in your life instead of focusing on what you don't have. As you begin to express your gratitude for all that you currently have, you effectively open the door for even greater abundance to manifest in your life.

The key is to make the expression of gratitude a daily ritual for you, remembering to be thankful upon awakening, throughout the day, and just prior to falling asleep as well. The point is, to become more conscious of the various blessings that you receive each day, rather than simply taking them for granted.

The second suggestion, related to abundance, is to recognize the importance of the act of *giving* itself. As we give, so shall we receive, but this age-old adage does not mean the God-Force keeps score of how much you give in order to identify the amount you should receive in return. The relationship between giving and receiving actually ties back to the principles of *Cause and Effect* and *Oneness* that were discussed in earlier chapters.

Every cause that you initiate leads to an effect; therefore when you give you set energy into motion that must find its way back to you in one form or another. The key determinant of what returns, is the intent that was behind the original act of giving. If it was truly a sincere gift, then one cannot help but receive something positive in return.

Oneness relates to 'giving and receiving' in a very basic way. If we are all part of the same energy field, then by definition anything that we give to another – in a heartfelt way – we actually give to ourselves as well.

In this chapter, we also learned that perhaps the worst kind of gift you can give is one that is given so "you don't have a bad feeling." Giving cannot be a positive experience when the underlying motivation for it is a feeling of obligation or guilt. That is why it's necessary to set standards for yourself with respect to all of your giving practices, and this includes establishing guidelines for donating money to charitable institutions. Once you have done this, it is also essential to discipline yourself to give as a matter of routine.

The third suggestion regarding the principle of abundance is to recognize that it is important for you to actually *spend* money. This does not mean that you should use money recklessly by piling up debt and depleting savings, but rather that it is necessary for you to learn to use money, without the fear of not having enough of it in the future.

Remember, whenever you make the decision to invest in anything that you feel strongly about having or doing, no matter how inexpensive or costly, you are showing your faith that the Universe will in turn provide you with opportunities to experience even greater abundance.

Finally, the fourth suggestion related to the principle of abundance is to understand how critical it is for you to be *doing what you love*. As you do, you effectively tap into the energy of your Higher Self, and in the process allow your limitless 'I' to fully express itself rather than your fearful, self-conscious 'me'. When you are doing something you love, you step outside of your active conscious mind because you are not really thinking about what you're doing, but rather you are 'feeling' it.

Every person in this world does indeed have unique, innate skills that literally crave to be expressed. If you don't believe this is true, remember that the God-Force has never made two people exactly alike. If you feel that there is no way anyone would pay you for doing whatever it is that you love, or that there is limited opportunity in that particular field, think again.

When you make the choice to do what you love, you move into right alignment with the Universe, which consequently allows you to draw to yourself all sorts of new positive energies and opportunities. Nonetheless, if you cannot picture yourself leaving behind the elusive safety of your existing profession, then it is crucial for you to at least develop a more positive attitude regarding it.

This chapter also touched upon the subject of money, stressing the necessity of coming to the understanding that, at its most fundamental level, money is simply another form of energy; it is not by any means abundance itself. So, while money is undoubtedly a vital commodity in modern society, you need to keep it in perspective by acknowledging that it is merely one aspect of that which makes up an abundant life.

It is also important for you to take an inventory of your existing beliefs about money, for if you are like the average person, somewhere within your subconscious mind are negative beliefs that do not serve you in your efforts to achieve financial independence. It is therefore necessary that you first identify those beliefs, then begin to methodically dispute them, and finally make your best efforts to replace them with beliefs that are positive in nature.

This chapter likewise discussed a technique for disputing unwanted beliefs that is based on a type of psychotherapy called Rational-Emotive Therapy (RET). This technique calls for a scientific approach using reason, logic, and facts to counter 'irrational' beliefs.

Once you begin to liberate yourself from limiting beliefs about money, naturally you will need to replace them with more empowering alternatives. In that regard, it is a good idea to take the time to read a selection of spiritual growth books that have a focus on money or the principle of abundance. In addition, the regular use of affirmations helps to firmly implant new beliefs within your subconscious mind.

Whatever new beliefs about money you choose to adopt, make best efforts to remember that from your soul's point of view, the primary purpose for having money is to buy life experiences, as opposed to just collecting material goods.

Related Reading

Stuart Wilde, *The Little Money Bible*: Chapter 1

Richard & Mary-Alice Jafolla, *The Quest, A Journey of Spiritual Rediscovery*: Chapter 37

Dr. Wayne W. Dyer, *You'll See It When You Believe It*: Chapter 4

Arnold Patent, *You Can Have It All*: Giving and Receiving; Abundance

Deepak Chopra, *Creating Affluence*: Chapter 2

Stuart Wilde, *Infinite Self*: Step 15

Let's move on to Chapter 8 where the principle of Non-attachment is discussed in detail.

8: Non-attachment

To hold,
One must detach,
And to keep,
One must release.

TIBETAN MASTER
DJWHAL KHUL

The principle of *Non-attachment* states, that for you to obtain any-thing at all you must first give up your *attachment* to it, or *need* for it. In other words, you must drop your attachment to the outcome. There is also a second aspect to non-attachment, which is that in order to fully enjoy something or someone that is already in your life, you have to drop your attachment to it/them as well.

This principle tends to be more difficult for people in Western countries to accept, since many have been conditioned to embrace the 'make it happen' approach to life. Namely, using the sheer force of will to ensure that desires are fulfilled, and then fighting to hold on to whatever was acquired. Non-attachment, however, is about learning to trust in your real Self (i.e., your Higher Self), about going with the flow of life rather than trying to row your boat upstream. It is also about tapping into the power of the God-Force to attract literally anything you desire, and likewise it's about leaving behind the need to cling to what you already have.

Now if you are like most people in Western culture, it is likely that the idea of being detached and going with the flow wasn't part of your socialization process. So, to better understand non-attachment, let us take a moment to clarify what the term *attachment* actually means. To paraphrase Fr. Anthony DeMello, simply put, an attach-ment is an emotional state of clinging, caused by the notion that without some particular thing, person, affiliation, idea, belief or out-come, you cannot be happy.

THE PROBLEM WITH ATTACHMENTS

There are, in fact, two key problems with having attachments to people, things, and outcomes. First, if the object of a given attachment cannot be obtained, the result is unhappiness and perhaps downright misery for some folks. Second, even if one is able to obtain whatever or whoever to which they are attached, the result is not long-lasting happiness, but rather some fleeting amount of satisfaction followed by anxiety about losing it or them. Think about this for a moment: how many times in your life have you been motivated by a strong desire to have something or someone, or to achieve something, and then once your desire was satisfied, your concern shifted toward holding on to whatever it was?

The reality is that "*fear* and *insecurity*"[88] lie at the foundation of all material attachments. The need for security in particular is caused by the failure to remember who we really are: 'sparks of the Divine' that possess unlimited creative power. The true source of wealth, or anything else in the physical world is the pure consciousness underlying all form; the field of pure potentiality discussed in the previous chapter about abundance.

Attachment to anything at all in the world of form is an outward expression of a scarcity consciousness that resides *within* us. When we cling to things, what we effectively do is cut ourselves off from a whole range of other possibilities (i.e., abundance), yet the vast majority of us cannot seem to stop ourselves from doing so. We human beings do indeed have the tendency to develop a wide assortment of attachments. In the balance of this chapter, we will closely examine some of the more typical attachments, and also discuss the various benefits that one can accumulate by learning to leave them behind.

ATTACHMENTS TO PEOPLE

Developing attachments to other people is a common practice in virtually every culture throughout the world. This behavior is so

---

[88] Deepak Chopra, *The Seven Spiritual Laws of Success*, op. cit., p. 84

prevalent, that the mere mention of the concept of becoming more detached in human relationships can be met with severe disapproval. According to mainstream opinion, it is perfectly normal to need other people, for the basic reason that human beings are inherently social animals. While there is no disputing that we as a species are gregarious in nature, there is a big difference between preferring the company of others, and actually *needing* it.

From my experience, attachments to people can have up to three different elements. First, there is the attachment to an individual person as the object of one's affection (i.e., a romantic partner). Second, there is the attachment to a rigid code defining how we believe persons to whom we are attached should think, behave and conduct their lives (i.e., a *need* for the person to think and behave in a certain way). Third, there is the attachment to obtaining approval from a person (or persons) to whom one feels attached. Some relationships have just one of these elements, while others may have two or all three. Let us now look at each of them in some greater detail.

Attachment to a Romantic Partner

Whenever we become attached to someone as a romantic partner, there tends to be a strong inclination for us to become focused on how to hold on to that person, rather than simply enjoying his or her company in the present moment. In essence, what occurs is that we move from a feeling of wanting that person to one of needing him or her. This is because most of us have been conditioned since we were children to believe that we *must* have a partner in life in order to make ourselves complete. I can testify that in my experience this is true. I vividly recall hearing many people tell me over the years that finding 'that special someone' was the key to my long-term happiness.

Our culture's fascination with romantic love is really quite pervasive. If you have any doubts about this, just listen to many of the most popular songs during the past fifty years or more, and you will hear all kinds of lyrics about how badly someone needs someone else, (e.g., "Baby I need your lovin'," or "If you leave me now, you'll take away the biggest part of me," and so on).

We are literally bombarded with this type of programming in music, and in films, books and TV shows as well. In view of these messages, it is not surprising that so many people develop the belief that they need a romantic partner in their life. The reality is that whenever you approach a love relationship from a position of need, you are actually putting yourself into a very uneasy position.

In particular, if you come to believe that you truly need another person to be fulfilled, you can never rest easy because there is always the possibility they may have a change of heart and leave, or worse yet, die. That is why the age-old advice that we should first be able to live happily on our own is so very practical. Some might say that attachment is unavoidable in love relationships, and in most friend-ships as well, but as this next passage from Arnold Patent illustrates, this is not necessarily so:

> *You can have a relationship with a person,*
> *have total commitment to the relationship,*
> *trust the other person completely and yet have no attachment*
> *to the person or to the relationship.*
> *You give the other person total freedom at all times.*
> *The relationship continues as a result of the participants*
> *reconfirming the relationship, constantly.*[89]

From my own life experience, it is indeed possible to develop the type of relationship that Mr. Patent describes above. During our eleven years of marriage, both my wife and I have maintained such a spirit of detachment within our union. While we do love each other dearly, at the point from which we became seriously involved, we have always remained cognizant of the fact that in addition to our life together, we also have independent lives (i.e., we are not "joined at the

---

[89] Arnold Patent, *You Can Have It All,* op. cit., p. 60

hip"). For example, on more than one occasion, we have even taken brief vacations on our own. The secret of our success, if you will, is that we literally do reconfirm our relationship on a continual basis.

Now, if I can approach a love relationship in this way, anyone can, because for years I was a die-hard romantic idealist that always developed attachments. Should you elect to adopt a more detached approach to your own close personal relationships, you may find yourself amazed at the increase in joy and satisfaction that can be experienced.

Attachment to How Someone Should Think and Behave

Any time we choose to become attached to a romantic partner, a friend, or a relative, it is also very common for us to develop an attachment to how we believe that person should think, behave and conduct their life. Because we care about them, perhaps we also feel we have the right to establish an unbending, arbitrary set of standards for them, or maybe our affection leads us to assume we know what is best for them. Whatever the reason, this type of attachment always returns to us some level of emotional trauma. Why? People inherently do not like to be told what to think and how to act.

When you practice detachment in personal relationships, it does not in any way mean that you become disinterested in the person's welfare. The fundamental difference in your approach is that you do not force-feed your philosophy and/or opinions to people, nor do you attempt to manipulate them in any way. In adopting a non-attached perspective, you learn to accept people as they are, while at the same time reserving the right to provide them with constructive guidance.

Attachment to Approval from Others

This type of attachment can occur in any sort of relationship, including associations of both a personal and professional nature. As discussed in Chapter 3, the vast majority of us have been conditioned from birth to seek approval from outside ourselves. Naturally some people are more approval-oriented than others, but in my estimation there is probably only a tiny percentage of the population that has little or no attachment to outside approval.

As with other attachments, this type also has both positive and negative elements to it, in that it always feels great when you get the 'stroke', but that thrill quickly fades and leaves you anxious for the next dose. Needing approval from others actually puts you into a very uncomfortable position, simply because you can never really relax when you have to keep looking over your shoulder to see if you are 'making the grade'. Moreover, as mentioned previously, whenever you are outer (or other), rather than inner-directed, your happiness is totally outside of your control because you are, in effect, a slave to public opinion, and that is a high-stress place to be in.

The only way out of this trap is to detach from the *need* to be acknowledged or approved of in any way. You accomplish this by learning to drop your emotional need for receiving approval, and replace it with an unemotional preference. In other words, you come to the point where if you meet with someone's approval, great; if you don't, then 'so it goes'.

While this takes a certain amount of discipline and practice, the payoff for adopting this attitude is substantial. As a former 'approval-hound', I can readily speak from experience on this topic, for once I dropped my *need* for outside approval in both my personal and professional lives, either the quality of a relationship improved, or the relationship faded away.

In particular, those individuals who were previously annoyed by my neediness now sensed a positive change in me and responded accordingly. Additionally, those who had used my need for approval to manipulate me were no longer able to, so they either adjusted their behavior, or eventually moved on out of my life. The reason for all of this was very basic, letting go of the need for approval actually changed the nature of the energy signals that I was emitting.

Once you, too, make the decision to drop all need for approval from your spouse, partner, family, friends, work associates and superiors, I am confident that you'll experience similar positive changes in your life as well.

ATTACHMENT TO OWNING THINGS

Among most people, there is a strong attachment to owning things. The United States has especially become a consumption-based society, one in which many have actually come to believe that what you own is who you are. This same attitude is steadily being exported to second and third world countries as well.

Please don't misunderstand me here. There is nothing wrong at all with people buying material goods (i.e., nonessential items) when they feel like doing so – I most certainly do. Problems are bound to develop however, when that feeling is based on an ill-founded premise that continuing to purchase such things will actually provide them with genuine happiness, security, or even improved social status.

From Main Street to Wall Street to Washington,
From men to women to men
It's a nation of noses pressed up against the glass
They've seen it on the TV
And they want it pretty fast.[90]

DON HENLEY
"GIMME WHAT YOU GOT"

During an average month in the United States, we are barraged with literally thousands of messages originating from a variety of sources, the majority of which are designed to get us to buy either a product or an idea. As a result of this media-driven culture, we have millions of people taking on significant amounts of debt just so they can 'own' and become attached to and/or burdened by more and more stuff.

---

[90] Don Henley, Stan Lynch and John Corey, Copyright © 1988 Cass County Music/Matanzas Music (ASCAP) (All rights reserved. Used by permission.) From the CD *The End of the Innocence*, (The David Geffen Company, manufactured exclusively by Warner Bros. Records, Inc., a Time Warner Company. 1988).

The "More" Disease

I used to participate in a bit of that behavior myself, until one day when I heard Dr. Wayne Dyer talk about the disease called *more*. This serious affliction results from having a thought like, "I know I'll be happier or feel more fulfilled if I just have a new home, or car, or stereo, etc." The reality is that as long as we believe that we need something outside of ourselves to bring us happiness, we will constantly have to buy more things, and that, my friend, is an endless trap.

What we usually get with minor purchases – at best – is a thrill that is invariably temporary in nature. With larger and more costly purchases (i.e., homes, cars), we can derive benefits over a longer period of time, but these benefits are often more than offset by the reduced personal freedom that results from increasing our financial commitments. That, combined with the increased anxiety we experience about holding onto and protecting these possessions, makes the total price we pay even higher.

This does not mean that you need to stop being a consumer of anything other than essential items, for as we learned in Chapter 7, it is important for you to keep money circulating in your life. Rather, what you need to do is come to the understanding that whatever you buy is meant to serve *you* in some way, and that at the most fundamental level you never really own anything in the first place — you just *use* it. This is because even if you hold the title to something, the fact that you will not live forever means that you never truly *own* it, since at the moment of your death it will be passed on to someone else anyway.

This is not to suggest that you shouldn't appreciate or take care of the various goods that you purchase, for it is both sensible and practical that you do. What is important however, is to not get so focused on protecting and caring for your possessions that the stuff itself begins to control you.

Like many people, I can speak from experience about this. I used to be obsessed about the safety and appearance of my automobiles.

Back in 1990, for example, after my new Honda Prelude was van-
dalized outside my workplace, I promptly purchased a state-of-the-
art car alarm to serve as a deterrent to any other such incidents. I
even made it a practice to poke my head out of the front door of the
office now and then and check to see if the car was still safe. As I
write this, more than ten years later, it is actually somewhat comical
to me that I could have even allowed myself to be that controlled by
a material item.

Today, I cannot even imagine behaving in the same manner, for
my consciousness was forever altered once I came to accept the principle that it isn't possible for me to truly own anything in the first
place. This does not in any way imply that I don't care for the two
cars and the home that we currently use, because I most assuredly
do. The difference is that while it remains likely that I would still be
somewhat upset by theft or damage to these items, I know for certain that any negative feelings I'd experience would more than likely
be fleeting in nature.

The Cost of Clinging

It takes considerable energy to cling to things, and equally as
important: by being attached we serve to limit the flow of universal
energy into our lives. In that regard, consider this insightful and
very amusing quotation from Stuart Wilde:

> *The more you defend your stuff through the emotion of "mine,"*
> *the more lack you'll have, and the more you cut yourself off*
> *from the Infinite Self within. Everything you have is in the*
> *care of the God Force. If you come home and the stereo*
> *is missing, you can say, "Ah, they've come for the stereo,"*
> *rather than getting uptight. It's just gone back to the*
> *God Force. Somebody else has it now.*[91]

While the previous passage has a humorous nature, it really is

---

[91] Stuart Wilde, *Infinite Self*, op. cit., p. 130–131

quite true in my view. Once an item of yours is taken from you, what else can you do but accept it? Getting all bothered about it does not in any way change what happened. This is not to suggest that thieves should not be held responsible for their choices. Rather, it means that those who were victimized need to first reframe the event (e.g., as a lesson learned), and then move into the present moment to identify the appropriate solution (e.g., file a police report, purchase a new stereo, or both).

If you are sincerely able to embrace this perspective, you will eventually reach the point where you no longer allow yourself to become rigidly attached to any material item. The end result will be a feeling of immense weight being removed from your shoulders, as the emotional and physical energy that you invest in hanging on to your stuff literally weighs you down. Most importantly, as you begin to develop the ability to be non-attached and let things flow *from* your life without resistance, you simultaneously crack open the door for new items to flow *into* your life.

ATTACHMENT TO TRADITION

This attachment is perhaps at the root of more conflict in the world than anything else. If you doubt this to be true, take a moment to consider most of the ongoing struggles in world, and you will find that 'tradition' has something to do with them.

For example, there are the much-publicized problems between the Arabs and Israelis in the Middle East, and the skirmishes between the Catholics and the Protestants in Northern Ireland, and of course there are the centuries-old differences between the various factions within the former Yugoslavia. Add to that the continuing rift between Russia and the Republic of Chechnya, and the longstanding division between the Greeks and Turks: need I go on here?

If you look closely at each of these conflicts, as well as others around the globe, you will find that several are occurring today because of some event or events that happened long ago, or as a result of some established cultural or religious teaching. More often than not folks are fighting about something that has absolutely nothing to do with the present moment! Interestingly, nobody on either side of the conflict stops to think about how illogical this behavior is, because they are simply too emotionally 'wired-in' as a result of their conditioning.

Just because the people of a neighboring nation did some nasty deeds to your ancestors, or happen to practice a different religion than you, does not by any means justify going into battle against them today. The common retort to such a comment is that it is merely part of heritage of the various peoples; it cannot be helped: it is based on wounds that have festered over the centuries, blah, blah, blah.

Yet, if you were to put a Jewish baby into a playpen with a Palestinian baby, or a Kosovar baby with a Serbian baby, it's quite likely after some initial sorting out occurs that harmony would be the order of the day. In any event, they surely wouldn't feel inspired to *kill* each other.

The way out of this attachment to tradition is obvious, and that is for adults to stop passing these negative teachings on to their off-spring. The problem is that it is very difficult to break the chain, because leaving behind custom and tradition also means abandoning the safety and comfort associated with being an accepted member of the society or culture. This is the primary reason that conflicts among ethnic groups and nations continue to persist, as it takes quite a bit of determination to forsake these old teachings and customs.

Should you find yourself on either side of such a conflict, it can be helpful to ask yourself why you continue to foster an attachment to the past. You can elect, instead, to mine the pure potential of this moment and create an entirely different, more positive reality.

ATTACHMENT TO RELIGIOUS CUSTOMS

If we look more closely at religious customs, we can see how attachments to them can have a very negative effect on a person's spiritual growth potential. Specifically, as discussed in Chapter 2, organized religion essentially wraps things up in a tight package that requires little if any contemplation on the part of the individual church member. While this tends to simplify life, it clearly limits one's ability to strike out and discover his or her own perception of the truth. Moreover, when someone in the congregation does choose to pursue a different path, the response from those remaining firmly in the fold, especially parents, relatives, and friends, is generally not very positive.

If you are a person that truly wants to explore new spiritual path(s), recognize right now that you simply need to drop any concerns that you may have about what those who remain firmly attached to religious traditions will think of you. If you are ever to come to a meaningful awareness of who you really are, you must be willing to leave no stone unturned in your quest.

ATTACHMENT TO OTHER CUSTOMS

Attachments to other customs abound in our world, as the passing on of various traditions, as well as beliefs, is part and parcel of every culture on the planet. The problem is, that being unquestioningly attached to such customs and beliefs also has the tendency to limit one's ability to discover his or her own inner truth. Let's take a closer look now at one example of a tradition to which people often become attached: that of identifying themselves with their nationality or race.

While there is certainly nothing at all wrong with being proud of one's physical and ancestral heritage, there are times when such identification can inhibit one's personal and/or spiritual growth. Just take a moment to reflect on some of what you were taught as a child regarding your nationality or race, and I am sure you will agree that some aspects of that curriculum were not all that inspiring.

As hypothetical examples, consider teachings such as, "You can't help being emotional and hotheaded dear, it is part of the very fabric of being Italian," or "Remember to be careful out there son, for it's still a white man's world." Advice or observations of this nature are usually passed on from generation to generation, with the purpose being to prepare the child or adolescent for the road ahead. While the intention is good, the concern is that much of what is passed on is not necessarily factual, nor is it typically constructive in nature.

Accordingly, when people accept such information without any real contemplation, they are simply buying into someone else's idea of truth rather than discovering their own. So, in the end you can still be proud of your heritage, but always remember that the real you is *not* your nationality or your race, nor is it a requirement that you embrace any of the customs or conventions associated with either of them.

This same principle applies with other traditions to which you adhere (e.g., those related to family or to memberships in organizations): never identify your essential self – who you really are – with them.

ATTACHMENT TO BEING RIGHT

This attachment can be found in societies throughout the world. As a particularly obvious example, just think back to the aftermath of the U.S. presidential election of 2000, when on essentially every news outlet one could find a voice for each political party, both of which believed that their side's position on the voting controversy was absolutely correct. Moreover, just tune in to any of a dozen or more nationally syndicated TV talk shows and you will find audiences full of people who truly believe that they, and only they, are 'right'.

Conflict and the Need to be Right

The 'need' to be right brings a whole lot of unnecessary conflict and misery into people's lives and relationships. However, most of us habitually fall prey to this attachment, simply because it is so easy to get caught up in thinking that our beliefs or views are superior to those of others.

To leave this tendency behind, it is necessary for you to practice remaining open-minded (see Chapter 1) regarding the ideas and viewpoints of others, by actually *listening* to differing views without immediately shutting them out. It is likewise important for you to put forth your best efforts to overcome the temptation to try to convince others of the rightness of your position.

ATTACHMENT TO THE PHYSICAL BODY

An attachment to maintaining or improving one's physical appearance will always lead to anxiety and disappointment, for the simple reason that the human body is constantly in a state of change. Despite this obvious fact, each year millions of people spend literally billions of dollars worldwide in an effort to either obtain or preserve a more youthful and attractive physical appearance.

To clarify, I am not referring to a fundamental caring for the body through exercise, proper diet, and grooming, or cosmetic surgeries required as a result of illnesses, accidents, or other traumas. I am referring to those nonessential medical procedures: (i.e., face lifts, tummy tucks, liposuction, breast implants, and so on) that are designed to improve body appearance as a means of enhancing self-esteem. The key problem with these types of procedures is that they are grounded in the premise that our external packaging *is* who we are.

As we learned in Chapter 3, what you really are is a divine spark of God, an eternal being who inhabits a particular physical body for a finite period of time. You are therefore a *spiritual being* having a *human experience,* and your body is the means for both experiencing this planet and expressing yourself. So while you must never forget that your body is a miraculous creation that deserves proper care and respect, also remember to avoid becoming attached to its appearance. Your continually changing body is merely a container that houses the real you — your Spirit.

ATTACHMENT TO WINNING

An attachment to winning is pervasive throughout the world. In the United States in particular, children are taught very early on about the importance of winning in their scholastic, athletic and other endeavors. The need to compete and win is then reinforced through-out adolescence and adulthood as well. Admonitions about how competitive things are in the real world are part of that training; so much so that by the time most children are in first grade they have been instilled with a strong desire to outperform their classmates.

This focus on competing is pervasive in literally all aspects of American life, and the result is a society in which the majority of people are fixated on winning. Just tune in and watch any sporting event on TV, and you will see both the thrill of victory and the agony of defeat etched in the faces of competitors and spectators alike. America does indeed spell competition, and the only way to the proverbial top is by winning. What is unfortunate, however, is that along with this preoccupation with winning comes a fair share of misery, for the simple reason that one quite obviously cannot win all the time.

There really is nothing wrong with having the desire to win in any area of life, but in your efforts to grow spiritually, your mission is to come to the awareness where you no longer feel an obsession to win. To accomplish this requires you to drop much of what you learned about competition earlier in life.

Perhaps most importantly, it is necessary to leave behind the age-old teaching that competition is required simply because there are only so many opportunities in this world. As we learned in Chapter 7, this world by its very nature is abundant, so there really is no need to compete with anyone unless you *believe* that you must. According to the renowned spirituality author Emmet Fox:

> *God never repeats Himself, and so He has never made*
> *two people alike, and it is for this reason that no two people*
> *could ever do the same work, or express themselves in quite the*
> *same way. That is why, rightly understood,*
> *there really need be no competition.*
> *There need be no such thing as, say, two thousand people*
> *struggling for the same place in life. Whatever the place may be,*

there can be only one person who can fill it perfectly;
and there are one thousand, nine hundred and ninety-nine
other places somewhere waiting for the people
if only they will find them.[92]

Once you can embrace the wisdom and practicality in Mr. Fox's words, then it will not be a stretch for you to see that it really isn't necessary for you to compete with any person for scholastic, employment, or other career/business opportunities.

The truth is that you *do* have unique capabilities that make you ideally suited for a certain station in life. Your primary task, then, is to first discover what they are, and then use them in ways that are both fulfilling to you, and of service to others.

Some might contend that you cannot completely remove competition from human interaction, particularly with respect to both amateur and professional athletics or sporting events. Granted, there can only be one winner in any given contest, but once again the key point is that even within this arena what is necessary is for you, as a participant, to drop the need to win.

Moreover, it is also prudent that you to learn to shift your perspective away from competing against another person, and instead toward competing against yourself. Those who participate in sports requiring one-on-one match-ups might disagree with this latter suggestion. However, if one gets down to the heart of the matter, our greatest challenge is always found in overcoming our own tendency not to do our very best in all of our endeavors.

Before leaving this subject, I will share with you a classic quotation regarding the danger of needing to win from a revered Chinese sage named Tranxu:

When the archer shoots for no particular prize,
he has all his skills; when he shoots to win a brass buckle,

---

[92] Emmet Fox, *Your Heart's Desire*, (Marina del Rey, CA: DeVorss & Co., 1933) p. 2–3

he is already nervous; when he shoots for a gold prize,
he goes blind, he sees two targets, and is out of his mind.
His skill has not changed, but the prize divides him.
He cares. He thinks more of winning than of shooting,
and the need to win drains him of his power.

ATTACHMENT TO MONEY

You think a little more money
can buy your soul some rest,
you better think of something else instead.[93]

TRIUMPH
"FIGHT THE GOOD FIGHT"

Conduct a poll worldwide regarding money beliefs, and the results would likely indicate that the majority of civilized populations share the conviction that having more money equals greater security. Unfortunately, as this excerpt from Dr. Deepak Chopra's *The Seven Spiritual Laws of Success* affirms, there is a fatal flaw in this commonly held belief about money:

Those who seek security chase it for a lifetime
without ever finding it. It remains elusive and ephemeral,
because security can never come from money alone.
Attachment to money will always create insecurity
no matter how much money you have in the bank.
In fact, some of the people who have
the most money are the most insecure.[94]

The desire for greater amounts of money is actually another

---

[93] Triumph, *Fight the Good Fight*, Copyright © 1981, BMG Careers Music Incorporated (All rights reserved. Used by permission.) From the album/CD *Allied Forces*, (TRC Records. 1981).

[94] Deepak Chopra, *The Seven Spiritual Laws of Success*, op. cit., p. 85–86

manifestation of the 'more' disease, which was discussed earlier in this chapter. The nagging feeling that 'if I just have more money I'll feel secure', is one that is shared by millions of people around the world. Yet Dr. Chopra is correct. If you were to interview a number of wealthy people, I believe you'd find that several of them would still express feelings of uneasiness about their long-term security.

As a person who has dealt with an attachment to money for many years, I can assure you that having more of it does not actually help you to feel more secure. In truth, even though my wife and I have more money today than we've ever had, I still continue to experience feelings of insecurity. Perhaps a key reason these feelings emerge is that the life of self-employment typically leads to my earning varying amounts of income each week.

Whatever the reason, thankfully I have made solid improvement in detaching from the need to acquire more money. Yet, I must admit that it has been, and continues to be a very challenging process for me. What I believe ultimately helped me most to see the value in detaching from money, was taking that four-month sabbatical to Greece mentioned in the previous chapter on abundance.

Whenever you feel that you simply *must* have more money to feel content or secure, somewhere within your consciousness are beliefs that are not rooted in abundance. If this is the case, then I suggest you first undertake the effort to identify those limiting beliefs, and then go about disputing them using the RET technique described in Chapter 7, or by employing a comparable approach.

As you embark on this process, please remember to be patient with yourself; completely leaving behind the attachment to money can indeed be very difficult, and particularly so if you happen to live within money-obsessed Western culture.

ATTACHMENT TO SECURITY

As referenced in the previous section, security (or certainty) is a very elusive concept, yet most people tend to crave it in a very intense way. From farm and factory workers to professional athletes making millions of dollars a year, we tend to hear the same refrain; "I just want a job or career situation that allows me to provide security for both myself and my family." If we were to dig a little deeper into that desire, we would find that a strongly held fear about what the future holds underlies it.

Driving this fear is the fact that human beings, for the most part, have a very powerful desire to be in full control of their lives. Dealing with uncertainty is quite a stressful experience for most people; to reduce their anxiety they undertake efforts to bring some level of security to their existence. As this next passage from Deepak Chopra indicates, however, their efforts in this regard are, in reality, misdirected:

> *The search for security is an illusion.*
> *In ancient wisdom traditions, the solution to this whole dilemma*
> *lies in the wisdom of insecurity, or the wisdom of uncertainty.*
> *This means that the search for security and certainty*
> *is actually an attachment to the known.*[95]

It actually is very true: people *are* attached to the 'known' because, as a rule, none of us really like change. We all tend to prefer the status quo because it's predictable, and therefore theoretically safe. This is the case even if we are not content with our present situation, for in a very real sense it is preferable to have the certainty even at the price of unhappiness.

There is however, a big problem that arises from attachment to the 'known': it may well prevent us from experiencing all sorts of wonderful and positive things out there in the 'unknown'. As Joseph Campbell was heard to say, "nothing is exciting if you know what the outcome is going to be," and yet most people continue to crave predictability and certainty instead.

---

[95] Ibid., p. 86

Overcoming the Need for Security

To overcome this particular attachment, you must first come to the decision that you are indeed willing to leave behind the alleged safety of the 'known'. The next step is to move beyond simply being willing, and actually venture into the 'unknown'. This action requires some courage on your part, and it's also necessary that you have some patience with yourself, for your desire for security was taught to you very early in life and then regularly reinforced as you matured. This craving is merely a bad habit, and as everyone knows, habits can be broken. In that regard, consider this additional excerpt from Stuart Wilde's *Infinite Self*:

> One of the ideas to remember is that the need to feel
> secure is only a bad habit. You can feel secure even when
> you don't know what will happen next.
> It's only a custom of ego that requires you to "need to know."
> You don't! When you become more infinite
> in your perception, you become more open,
> and knowing what will happen next becomes
> less important. It's the difference between flow and restriction.
> You can be quite secure even when you don't know. [96]

Overcoming this habit essentially means leaving your old fear-based conditioning behind by learning to trust in the very force that created you. The best way to accomplish this, is to adopt the "let go and let God" attitude discussed in Chapter 2: *Who or What is God?* This means *surrendering* the 'need to know' that Mr. Wilde refers to in the preceding passage, to a higher power.

In my own life, I will admit that in the past I have found this process to be very testing, because my formative years were filled with regular admonitions about the importance of pursuing securi-

---

[96] Stuart Wilde, Infinite Self, op. cit., p. 78

ty. Nonetheless, I have remained on my own uncharted path of spiritual growth because my intuition tells me this *is* what I am supposed to be doing, and many things continue to show up in my life to confirm this.

From all that I have witnessed, successfully dealing with uncertainty requires that you keep your thoughts in the present moment as much as possible, for normally it is only when you are 'time-traveling' into the future that insecurity besets you. While you cannot actually stop the fear-based future thoughts that emerge within your consciousness, you can develop the skill to witness those thoughts instead of identifying with them, and then remind yourself to return to the present moment.

You might be thinking, "Hey, that's going to take a lot of effort," and if that is your reaction, you are absolutely correct. It is definitely not easy to become a more conscious being, but just what is your alternative? Sure, you can always keep doing what you are doing, but if it hasn't brought you the happiness and fulfillment that you've desired, then why not learn to better exercise God's greatest gift to you besides life itself—*freewill choice.*

This ability to freely choose to what you give your thought and feeling energy means that you do not have to stay the same way you have always been; you can instead leave behind those aspects of your conditioning that merely serve to limit your potential to experience joy in this life.

To end this discussion about the attachment to security, I ask that you take a moment to reflect upon this very inspiring and practical passage from Deepak Chopra:

When you experience uncertainty,
you are on the right path—so don't give up.
You don't need to have a complete and rigid idea of what
you'll be doing next week or next year,
because if you have a very clear idea of what's going to happen

> *and you get rigidly attached to it,*
> *then you shut out a whole range of possibilities.*[97]

ACCEPTING NON-ATTACHMENT

If you find yourself struggling in any way to accept the principle of non-attachment, don't fret over it, because it really is quite a radical teaching compared to what most of us have been taught.

To further build a case for the validity of this principle, I will close this chapter with another of my favorite quotes regarding this subject; this one is from Arnold Patent:

> *Noticing the way the Universe functions and using It*
> *as a model leads us to conclude that the ideal state*
> *is freedom of movement. Air moves freely*
> *through the atmosphere. Water flows freely*
> *down rivers and streams. Waves roll freely*
> *onto beaches. The earth moves freely*
> *on its axis. So it is with the affairs of humans.*[98]

In the workings of the Universe-at-large, there is no attachment to anything, just an effortless unfolding and a total focus on the present moment. You, too, are part of that Universe, so in truth it is your natural state as well to be non-attached and fully in the flow of life.

SUMMING IT ALL UP

The principle of non-attachment states that in order to obtain anything in the physical universe, you must first give up your *attachment* to it (or *need* for it). Additionally, to fully enjoy something or someone that is currently in your life, you must drop your attachment to it or them as well. To be fully detached means to trust in your true Self, and to go with the flow of life rather than against it.

An attachment is an emotional state of clinging caused by the

---

[97] Deepak Chopra, *The Seven Spiritual Laws of Success*, op. cit., p. 87–88
[98] Arnold Patent, *You Can Have It All*, op. cit., p. 59

notion that without some specific thing, person, affiliation, idea, belief or outcome a person cannot be happy. At the foundation of all attachments lies both fear and insecurity, with the need for security driven by our inability to remember the unlimited creative power that we all possess.

Developing attachments to people is prevalent in essentially every country throughout the world. This behavior is considered perfectly normal since humans are intrinsically social beings. While there is little doubt that humans desire interaction, there is in fact a large difference between desiring the company of others and actually needing it.

Attachments to people can have up to three different elements; they are: 1) attachment to a romantic partner, 2) attachment to how someone should think and behave, and 3) attachment to receiving approval from others.

Whenever there's an attachment to a romantic partner, it is very common for the person who is attached to become focused on holding onto that person, instead of simply enjoying their company in the present moment. The reality is that anytime you believe that you need someone else to be fulfilled, you can never rest assured, because there is always the possibility they may depart, or perhaps even die.

An attachment to a strict code regarding how someone should think, behave, and conduct their life will usually always return to you some level of emotional pain. While it's difficult to detach and let people be who they choose to be, not doing so will in the end lead to an increasing likelihood that conflict will develop. Becoming detached does not require that you stop caring; it actually means caring enough to approach the person with an attitude of total acceptance.

Attachment to receiving approval from others is a very common human trait. While it is always nice to get a positive 'stroke', the thrill quickly fades and leaves you craving for the next dose. Being outer-directed, therefore, means that your happiness is outside of your control, and that is not a very comfortable condition in which to live.

Within modern society as a whole, there is a strong attachment to owning things, and in many countries it has come to the point where many people now believe that what they own *is* who they are. This focus on consumption has led to an epidemic of the 'more' disease, a serious affliction that results from the belief that having additional 'things' will ensure happiness and/or fulfillment in life.

The point is not that you must stop purchasing nonessential items; instead, you should come to the awareness that what you buy is meant to serve you in some way, and not the other way around. It is likewise crucial to understand that you never really own anything, you just use it, simply because it always gets transferred to someone else eventually when you pass on.

It takes a lot of energy to cling to things, and when you do so, you also serve to restrict the flow of universal energy into your life. As you develop the ability to detach and let things flow from your life without opposition, you will simultaneously open the door for new items to enter.

Attachment to tradition is perhaps responsible for the majority of the planet's ongoing hostilities. As illogical as this is, the wars continue simply because most of the people involved are so emotionally conditioned that they literally "can't see the forest for the trees." The only way out of this dilemma is for adults to first come to a new awareness about tradition as it relates to conflict, and second, to stop passing on this conditioning to their children.

Attachment to religious customs can severely limit one's spiritual growth potential. Moving away from them, however, tends to be very difficult because of existing personal relationships with others involved in the faith. In order to explore a new spiritual path or paths however, it's necessary to drop any concerns about what anyone else will think.

Attachments to other customs are also prevalent throughout the world. The passing on of customs and beliefs is an integral part of every culture. The problem is that attachments to such traditions typically serve to limit a person's ability to discover his or her own truth.

The attachment to being 'right' is also widespread. Most people pick up this habit because it's very easy to fall into the trap of believing in the superiority of our beliefs or views. The way out of this attachment is to practice remaining open-minded when you encounter differing or opposing viewpoints, and to resist the temptation to justify your position.

An attachment to maintaining or improving physical appearance will always lead to anxiety and disappointment, simply because the human body is always changing. While it is appropriate to respect and care for the body, it's another thing altogether to invest in nonessential medical procedures as a means of enhancing self-esteem. Such procedures are based on the mistaken belief that the body we occupy *is* who we really are.

The attachment to winning is a worldwide phenomenon. Children are usually taught about the importance of competing and winning early in life, and that message is continually reinforced throughout adolescence as well as adulthood. While it is perfectly fine to have the desire to win, serious problems arise when one begins to feel they *must* win.

One of the keys to dropping this attachment is to leave behind the belief that you have no choice but to compete, given the generally held belief that there are only so many opportunities available in this world. This belief runs contrary to the principle of abundance, and it also fails to recognize that every person is uniquely qualified to fulfill a specific purpose in life.

Attachment to money is widespread throughout the civilized world, where millions of people mistakenly believe that having additional money will help them to feel happier or more secure. Unfortunately, chasing happiness or security by accumulating money is always futile, simply because neither of these feelings can come from money alone.

Attachment to security or certainty is quite prevalent across this entire planet. Despite being an elusive commodity, people literally crave security due to a deeply held fear of the future. The search for security and certainty is actually an attachment to the 'known'. People generally do prefer the status quo, even if they are not happy with it, for the simple reason that it's predictable and it feels safe. However, being attached to the known does have one major draw-back – it keeps us from experiencing all of the incredible things that could be out there in the 'unknown'.

One key to successfully dealing with uncertainty is to keep your thoughts centered in the present moment as much as possible, for feelings of insecurity are always related to the future. Although you cannot completely prevent fear-based thoughts from popping into your consciousness, with some conscious effort you can learn to wit-ness them instead of identifying with them.

If you have trouble accepting the principle of non-attachment, merely look at the Universe itself as the perfect example of effortless unfolding. As a part of that system, your natural state is likewise to 'go with the flow', and to be non-attached as well.

Related Reading

Stuart Wilde, *Infinite Self*: Step 7 & 15

Arnold Patent, *You Can Have It All*: Non Attachment

Deepak Chopra, *The Seven Spiritual Laws of Success*: Chapter 6

Dr. Wayne W. Dyer, *You'll See It When You Believe It*: Chapter 5

The topic of our next chapter is the principle of *Forgiveness*.

9: Forgiveness

There are people in your life,
Who've come and gone,
they've let you down,
You know they've hurt your pride,
You better put it all behind you,
because life goes on,
You keep carrying that anger,
It will eat you up inside.[99]

DON HENLEY
"THE HEART OF THE MATTER"

The term *forgiveness* is familiar to virtually all people, yet it is very likely that few truly understand its real meaning. Most individuals tend to regard forgiveness as being a truly magnanimous gesture on *their* part: one that is undertaken on behalf of the other person. Moreover, those individuals who, as rule practice forgiveness in their lives, tend to be viewed as upstanding human beings of great moral or spiritual fiber. While some folks may merit such lofty praise, the startling truth is that at its most fundamental level, forgiveness is more a *selfish* act than a noble one.

Now it wouldn't surprise me if you are somewhat shocked by the preceding statement, as it clearly runs contrary to conventional teaching on this topic. So for clarification purposes, it should be noted that the word 'selfish' when used in this context does not have a negative meaning. Extending forgiveness to someone is selfish in the sense that it is actually more beneficial to the person doing the forgiving, than it is to the person being forgiven.

The reason for this is quite simple—a sincere act of forgiveness

---

[99] Mike Campbell, Don Henley and J.D. Souther, Copyright © 1989 Cass County Music/Wild Gator Music/Ice Age Music (ASCAP) (All rights reserved. Used by permission.) From the CD *The End of the Innocence*, (The David Geffen Company, manufactured exclusively by Warner Bros. Records, Inc., a Time Warner Company. 1988).

allows us to release negative energy (i.e., excessive levels of adrenaline, other stress hormones) that can literally become toxic to the cells within our bodies. This next passage from *Discover the Power Within You* by Eric Butterworth supports this very point:

> *Actually, forgiveness is the simplest way*
> *to lighten our burdens. The man who forgives*
> *is no more saintly than one who insists upon keeping clean.*
> *In reality, the act of forgiveness constitutes*
> *a mental bath—letting go of something*
> *that can only poison us within.*[100]

Whenever we are unwilling to forgive, what we are doing is wasting a portion of our valuable present moment energy on something that no longer exists, except within the confines of our own mind. As we learned in Chapter 5, this backward 'time-traveling' is not the least bit empowering, for by drawing our attention from the 'now' it prohibits us from actually healing these outstanding issues and moving forward in life.

Within Western culture, it has only been of late that the medical establishment has begun to acknowledge that a connection does actually exist between the mind (and emotions) and a person's physical health. In Eastern tradition this connection has been an accepted truth for centuries. Among modern day personal/spiritual growth authors, Deepak Chopra has done an excellent job of bridging this gap between Eastern and Western medicine. This excerpt from his book *Ageless Body, Timeless Mind* is just one example of many that substantiate the impact that state of mind has on physical health:

> *Although the image of the body as mindless machine*
> *continues to dominate mainstream Western medicine,*
> *there is unquestionable evidence to the contrary.*
> *Death rates from cancer and heart disease are*

---

[100] Eric Butterworth, *Discover the Power Within You*, (New York, NY: HarperColllins Publishers, 1968) p. 154

provably higher among people in psychological distress,
and lower among people who have a strong sense of
purpose and well-being.[101]

Holding on to resentments (i.e., not forgiving) is also a form of psychological distress, for it is obviously a mental process rather than a physical one. Yet as you persist in clinging to your hurts by refusing to forgive, what you are actually doing is unconsciously storing negative energy within your body that may ultimately develop into some form of illness.

While some may doubt this, remember from Chapter 3 that every thought or feeling has within it the potential to manifest in some physical form. Unfortunately, because of the time it normally takes for the symptoms of a disease to develop, the vast majority of people have no clue that their own habitual negative thinking and feeling (or emotional) patterns may be at the foundation of their illness.

Some of the most compelling work in this area can be found in the writings of Louise Hay, an inspiring woman who literally healed herself of life-threatening cancer. Ms. Hay's *You Can Heal Your Life* is truly a classic book about the mind-body connection as it relates to physical health. Its basic premise is that human beings unconsciously create the 'illnesses' in their bodies, and that diseases originate from a state of unforgiving. As the following passage illustrates, Louise Hay makes it very clear that the key to healing is, in fact, forgiving:

We need to choose to release the past and forgive everyone,
ourselves included. We may not know how to forgive;
but the very fact we say we are willing to forgive
begins the healing process. It is imperative for our own
healing that "we" release the past and forgive everyone.[102]

So, if forgiveness does have such a positive effect on both emotion-

---

[101] Deepak Chopra, *Ageless Body, Timeless Mind*, op. cit., p. 20

[102] Louise Hay, *You Can Heal Your Life*, (Carson, CA: Hay House, Inc., 1984) p. 13

al and physical health, why is that most people have difficulty practicing it? One reason is that many continue to cling to old admonitions such as, 'an eye for an eye' or similar teachings. A second, and perhaps more prevalent reason is that by forgiving, one appears to *condone* whatever inappropriate behavior occurred.

As for the former reason, if you are a person that maintains 'an eye for an eye' philosophy, you might want to give some serious thought to this powerful Chinese proverb: "The one who pursues revenge should dig two graves." With respect to the latter reason, consider this insight from the best-selling author Caroline Myss:

> *Forgiving does not mean saying that what happened*
> *to you doesn't matter, or that it is all right for someone*
> *to have violated you. It simply means releasing*
> *the negative feelings you have about that event and*
> *the person or persons involved.*[103]

When you do opt to forgive a person or persons that have harmed you, or one or more of your loved ones in some way, you are by no means condoning what they did – not at all. What you *are* demonstrating by practicing forgiveness is that you will not allow your psyche and/or your body to be poisoned by the negative energy associated with holding on to resentments or grudges.

Another reason that people are reluctant to forgive is the misconception that practicing forgiveness requires them to actually communicate that sentiment on either a face-to-face or written basis. In a similar vein, there is also the mistaken belief that forgiving someone implies that the forgiver is willing to personally associate with that individual. From my experience, there is no absolute requirement that you must have any personal interaction with the person you are choosing to forgive, nor does forgiving someone mean that you are obliged to 'hang out' with that person.

---

[103] Caroline Myss, Ph. D., *Why People Don't Heal and How They Can*, (New York, NY: Harmony Books, 1997) p. 18

Instead of personal confrontation, you can extend your feelings of forgiveness using a prayer-based technique (one such method is discussed later in this chapter), or something similar, and in the process achieve the same beneficial results as if you had handled it personally. On the other hand, if you do feel a compelling desire to handle a given matter on a personal level, then I strongly recommend that before doing so you reflect upon this additional insight from Caroline Myss:

> *Should you need to contact anyone for a closure discussion,*
> *make sure that you are not carrying the message*
> *of blame as a private agenda. If you are, you are not genuinely ready*
> *to let go and move on. Should you need to share your closure*
> *thoughts in a letter to the person, do so, but again,*
> *make sure your intention is to retrieve your spirit from yesterday,*
> *not to send yet another message of anger.*[104]

IS ANYTHING UNFORGIVABLE?

There are probably millions of people who would say that the act of forgiving is nearly impossible in some circumstances, particularly when it comes to the perpetrators of heinous and/or violent crimes. While this position is of course very understandable, the fact is there is really nothing that cannot be forgiven, particularly when you fully comprehend that forgiving is about letting go of the toxic thoughts and emotions within *you*.

Without question, it is very difficult to forgive someone who has done something truly atrocious, yet holding on to judgment and anger can only bring greater discomfort. It may take a long time for a person to truly embrace forgiveness under such circumstances, but if one sincerely works at it long enough, they will eventually succeed in doing so. It is a matter of coming to the awareness that

---

[104] Caroline Myss, Ph. D., *Anatomy of the Spirit*, (New York, NY: Harmony Books, 1996) p. 216

forgiveness is really the only sensible option, for choosing the opposite course (i.e., holding on to resentment) carries with it the prospect of continued emotional suffering, and someday perhaps even severe physical pain as well.

Most everyone has seen the news media relate stories about people affected by violent crime who decide to visit a prison to forgive the person(s) responsible. These individuals are often portrayed as possessing almost a saint-like quality. The segments also tend to imply that what these folks did was well beyond what the average person could do. Yet as this passage from Dr. Joseph Murphy illustrates, every single one of us has the innate potential to behave in the exact same way, for the simple reason that forgiveness is as much a fundamental instinct for us as it is for the life force itself:

> *Life forgives you when you cut your finger.*
> *The subconscious intelligence within you sets about immediately*
> *to repair it. New cells build bridges over the cut. . . .*
> *Life holds no grudges against you,*
> *and it is always forgiving you.*[105]

Since all of us are individualized aspects of that life force (see Chapter 6, *Oneness*), we do indeed share its instinctive nature to forgive; it is simply a matter of learning to allow that higher aspect of ourselves to shine through the darkness caused by our conditioning. Granted, it can take a lot of practice on our part to learn to allow that natural instinct to express itself, but the potential payoffs (i.e., greater peace of mind, improved relationships, better health) are well worth the effort.

MY EXPERIENCE WITH FORGIVENESS

Prior to reaching my mid-thirties, I had no interest whatsoever in practicing forgiveness. Holding on to resentment and grudges was a

---

[105] Dr. Joseph Murphy, *The Power of Your Subconscious Mind*, op. cit., p. 181

way of life for me. Whenever any person did something to 'hurt' me I couldn't imagine just letting it go and moving on. There were even times I went as far as choosing to inflict some form of 'payback' just to let them know how lousy it felt. As I think back on that time of my life, I am almost amazed that I could have behaved in such destructive and heartless ways.

As with all major transformations that take place in a person's life, there is usually a watershed event, or a turning point if you will, that causes them to look at something in a totally different way. In my case, the attitude I held about forgiveness was altered more than a decade ago when I read the final chapter of Dr. Wayne Dyer's book *You'll See It When You Believe It*. Fittingly titled "Forgiveness," that chapter contained incredibly valuable and practical information to which I had never previously been exposed.

Today, some twelve years later, I still consider the material within that chapter to be the best I have ever read on this subject, and I strongly recommend it to anyone on the path of spiritual growth. There are in my view, a number of thought-provoking passages in that chapter, but the following one is perhaps most responsible for the significant change that occurred in my attitude about forgiveness:

> *Follow this logic. Someone has harmed you in some way*
> *in your past. You feel hurt and angry, and that anger*
> *ultimately turns to hatred. This is your hatred. You own it.*
> *It is you and you are it. The hatred is all thought,*
> *and is with you wherever you go. You have given someone*
> *permission not only to hurt you once, but to continue*
> *controlling your inner life. The hatred infects your life while*
> *the other person is still on his or her path*
> *doing exactly what he or she knows how to do,*
> *independent of your current miserable state.*[106]

---

[106] Dr. Wayne W. Dyer, *You'll See It When You Believe It*, op. cit., p. 251 - 252

As soon as I read those words, it was immediately obvious to me that Dyer was right. By holding on to resentment and bitterness, the only person I was hurting was myself, because whoever I felt hurt me had already moved on while I remained stuck in the past. It also occurred to me just how much energy I was wasting by hanging on to old hurts, so from that moment on I made the decision to work at dropping all of that old 'baggage'. Moreover, I made a promise to myself to no longer allow new feelings of anger or resentment to gain any sort of foothold in my consciousness.

As fate would have it, this shift in attitude would really prove beneficial a few years down the road when I was a partner in a small business that ultimately failed. For the sake of simplicity, let's just say that near the end of the company's life, the relationships that existed among the partners were not the least bit harmonious. What once could have been a great success, disappointingly never materialized. The end result was that fingers of blame were being pointed in all directions, and an overall feeling of mistrust was prevalent among all parties concerned.

Despite my intention to steer clear of resentment, I too, found myself beset by feelings of blame, anger and frustration. It was a very tough situation for everyone involved, and it became even more difficult after the doors were officially closed for the final time. That was because various legal issues related to the dissolution of the business eventually arose, and they would come to affect every partner involved. When the first set of such issues emerged, I was still dealing with nagging feelings of anger about what had occurred, and the net result was that I incurred a series of very expensive legal fees.

Thankfully, in the middle of that first round of legal activity I finally came to my senses, remembering all I had learned in Dyer's chapter about forgiveness. At that point I realized it was *my* responsibility to remove any lingering anger or resentment I had toward anyone involved in that venture. As I thought more about it, I just knew there had to be a spiritual solution for this problem; some technique I could apply to assist me in clearing out all of the negative feelings I was carrying around.

So I contacted a friend who had also been on the path of spiritual growth for some time, and she recommended that I add a forgiveness exercise to the 'quiet-time' that I was accustomed to taking on a daily basis. I was also encouraged to vividly picture each of my so-called adversaries, look them in the eye, and sincerely say, "I forgive you, and wish you nothing but peace." Recognizing the importance of leaving all of this negativity behind, I took to this exercise with fervent dedication, making it a part of my daily spiritual practice as prescribed.

Each day I completed the exercise with as much sincere *feeling* as I could, and by the time six months had elapsed, I can truthfully say I did not have a single ounce of animosity toward anyone involved in the situation. This did not mean that I wanted to see them, talk with them, or have anything at all to do with them ever again. It simply meant that I had left behind all of the negative feelings about them.

While I undertook this approach to the situation, I knew that others who were involved weren't addressing the matter in anywhere near the same way. That however, was not my concern. I simply went about living my life and had no interest whatsoever in participating in any additional conflict or negativity. Although there were still open issues to be resolved, from my perspective the matter was finished; I had in effect, already moved on. Interestingly, much later it came to my attention that a second round of legal activity had commenced, and strangely enough every single partner involved was required to participate - everyone that is, *except me.*

You might argue that it was merely a positive twist of fate, others that it was the result of human error, but they would never convince me that anything other than the sincere practice of forgiveness was responsible for what had occurred.

A HELPFUL FORGIVENESS PRAYER

During the past several years, I have had occasion to read a number of excellent spiritual growth books, and in one in particular I discovered a forgiveness prayer that both others and I have found to be very helpful. This prayer, which is printed directly below, comes from a very captivating book called *Awaken to the Healer Within*:

> *From the Divine Love that flows within my Being,*
> *I now call forth {insert name} to stand before me as*
> *I stand before you—in Love. I ask now that you forgive me*
> *as I forgive you. I embrace you in Love, and I thank you*
> *for the lessons that we have shared, but I now choose*
> *to release to the Light all bonds between us*
> *except those of unconditional love.*
> *I bid you to go in Peace. So be it!*[107]

When said with sincerity, this can be a very powerful prayer, one that I have seen work miracles in a person's life. For example, a very dear friend of mine – a truly wonderful person who had, unfortunately, been physically and emotionally abused throughout his childhood, successfully used it. As he grew into adulthood, the effect of this treatment manifested as problems with substance abuse, and an overall orientation toward over-indulgent behavior. As might be expected, his relationship with his parents was rooted in judgment and negativity, and although both his mother and father clearly knew that they played a part in his dysfunction, neither was capable of accepting any responsibility for it.

During the latter part of the 1990s, this gentleman made the decision to work at overcoming his addictions, and some time after that he recognized the importance of addressing the longstanding issues with his parents as well. One day during one of our frequent

---

[107] Rich Work w/Ann Marie Groth, *Awaken to the Healer Within*, (Mosinee, WI: Asini Publishing, 1995) p. 168–169

discussions, the subject of his parents came up again, so I took the opportunity to suggest that he begin using the aforementioned prayer every morning just as he awoke. My rationale was simple: he could never truly be free of all that stored negative emotion until he undertook the effort to forgive them. Surprisingly, he agreed with me fully, and promised to begin working with the prayer as suggested.

He worked with it for several months, and as time passed, little by little the chasm that existed between him and his parents narrowed. Today, several years later, the relationship between them is better than he ever thought it could be when he first embarked on this path of forgiveness. These results plainly demonstrate the power of this forgiveness prayer. If you find that you are truly willing to fully let go of a past hurt, then I strongly recommend that you apply it in your life as well.

THEY "KNOW NOT WHAT THEY DO"

As you undertake the effort to practice forgiveness in your life, it is also appropriate to take into consideration the words of Jesus as he neared his death, "Forgive them Father, for they know not what they do." Although this statement is familiar to many, I believe that most individuals would believe instead that those who harmed them were actually *well aware* of what they were doing.

From my experiences on this path, I've come to believe that a person who does harm to another is simply doing what they know how to do at the time given the level of their awareness of spiritual principles, nothing more, nothing less. While it can be difficult to adopt this perspective when an individual does something that is really mean or hurtful, if you got down to the heart of the matter, you would find they were merely doing the best they could in that moment to deal with *their own* life's issues and fears.

Think about it for a moment, and you realize that it is true; people (including you) are generally so focused on themselves and their own personal drama that they tend to be oblivious to what anyone else is going through at the time. That's why it is important for you not to take things personally, for people will be what people will be, and the underlying cause of their behavior actually has nothing to do with you. In that regard, consider this passage from a marvelous book called *The Four Agreements* by Don Miguel Ruiz:

> *Personal importance, or taking things personally,*
> *is the maximum expression of selfishness*
> *because we make the assumption that everything is about "me."*
> *Nothing other people do is because of you.*
> *It is because of themselves.*
> *All people live in their own dream, in their own mind;*
> *they are in a completely different world than the one we live in.*
> *When we take something personally, we make the assumption*
> *that they know what is in our world, and we try*
> *to impose our world on their world. Even when a situation*
> *seems so personal, even if others insult you directly,*
> *it has nothing to do with you.*[108]

When you can truly embrace this perspective, you will come to understand exactly what Jesus meant by "they know not what they do," and you'll also put yourself in a position where no one can ever really hurt you again. If you have any doubt that the latter can be true, then I strongly suggest that you read Ruiz's entire book, and pay particular attention to Chapter 3, "The Second Agreement: Don't Take Anything Personally."

FORGIVING YOURSELF

Many of us human beings have the tendency to be much harder on ourselves than we are on anyone else. We commonly feel remorseful about things we have said or done in the past, and at times those feelings become so intense that we actually begin to condemn ourselves. From my perspective, most of the guilt and the feelings of self-condemnation we experience are a complete waste of

---

[108] Don Miguel Ruiz, *The Four Agreements*, (San Rafael, CA: Amber-Allen Publishing, 1997) p. 48–49

energy, for what's done is truly done. The act of going back and repeatedly reliving the experience merely serves to take you out of the present moment, which as we learned in Chapter 5, is the only time that really exists in the first place.

The solution is therefore very simple: Learn to *forgive yourself* just as you forgive others, for you too were merely doing the best you knew how to do at that particular time. Equally as important, you need to develop the understanding that whatever did occur needed to happen for you to become the person you are today.

Easier said than done you might say, as self-forgiveness is not always a simple task, especially in the case of acts that caused significant pain or distress to other people. Nevertheless, if you aren't willing to release all of the resentment you feel toward yourself, how can you expect to be forgiven by whomever it is that you harmed? Moreover, without self-forgiveness, you simply cannot move forward in your spiritual growth, nor can you hope to succeed in your personal healing efforts.

To assist you in this process of forgiving yourself, I highly recommend the use of the following prayer, which I came across a few years ago. It is one that has always been of great value to me in my own efforts to release myself from past mistakes:

> *Spirit of the living God within, my precious holy Self,*
> *I totally and completely forgive myself for every thought,*
> *feeling, word, deed of the past. I release everything to you,*
> *all of my self-condemnation, all of my guilt, and all of my fear,*
> *and I close the door on all that was yesterday.*
> *As I forgive myself I know that I am forgiving all,*
> *for I am everyone, and everyone is me,*
> *and through the cleansing action of forgiveness*
> *we are all wonderfully free.*[109]

---

[109] John Randolph Price, *The Angels Within Us*, (New York, NY: Ballantine Books, 1993) p. 29

By saying this prayer each day with sincerity, I assure you that it will become increasingly easy for you to accept and approve of yourself, regardless of your past errors. So give it a try, my friend; what have you got to lose but some negative energy that can only harm you as you move forward in your life?

FORGIVENESS AND BLAME

As you continue along the path of spiritual growth, it is inevitable that you arrive at the point where you come to accept a simple but profound truth about forgiveness—that in order to forgive, you must first have assigned blame. Put another way, there is only a need to practice forgiveness when you fail to comprehend that at some level you are responsible for everything that you experience in life.

Coming to such a sophisticated level of awareness doesn't necessarily happen overnight. It is obvious that some really lousy things regularly happen to people who clearly would not have deliberately chosen to experience them. Yet as we learned in Chapter 4, literally everything that happens to us does originate from a cause that we *ourselves* put into motion through the energy signals (i.e., conscious and unconscious thoughts and feelings) we are always emitting.

What is unfortunate though, is that once again people are simply not conscious of all of the signals they are giving off, nor are most aware that they always have a choice as to how they process the behavior of others. The majority of human beings have trouble accepting the idea that they are actually responsible for the people, things and circumstances that show up in their lives. If you are a part of that majority, and happen to believe that the negative conditions you encounter are primarily the fault of *others*, then you need to understand that by assigning blame you are not in any way helping yourself.

When you blame other people, you effectively put both your feelings and your state-of-mind at the mercy of someone else's behavior (e.g., I'll be happy or satisfied when they apologize, or start or stop doing X or Y or Z, etc.). The better approach is for you to accept full responsibility for your life, adopting instead the perspective that it was *you* who attracted this negative person or situation to yourself so that you might learn a valuable lesson. It is from this position of personal power that true-life changes can occur.

To close this discussion about the principle of forgiveness, I will leave you with this additional thought-provoking passage from *Excuse Me, Your Life Is Waiting* by Lynn Grabhorn:

> *[True] forgiveness is about no longer holding onto or stewing over*
> *(focusing on) the thing that got us all riled up to begin with.*
> *And that holds true whether it happened five minutes*
> *or fifty years ago. Why? Because unless we let it go,*
> *we'll keep getting more of it, that's why.*
> *If we hold on to it, it's in our vibration.*
> *And if it's in our vibration, we're either going to attract it,*
> *or something similar in vibration. Over and over.*[110]

Ms. Grabhorn is correct, when you do make the choice *not* to forgive, you simply wind up storing negative energy within your consciousness, and that energy only serves to attract more of the same types of people and situations that brought pain or negativity to you in the first place. That is why it's so critical that you learn to forgive the past and completely let it go, for it *is* indeed already gone.

SUMMING IT ALL UP

The principle of forgiveness is a familiar but typically misunderstood concept, as most people tend to view it as a truly noble gesture on the part of the person doing the forgiving. The act of forgiving is actually a very selfish gesture, in that it provides you with the valuable opportunity to release toxic, negative feelings. Forgiveness essentially allows you to lighten your emotional burdens, and draws

---

[110] Lynn Grabhorn, *Excuse Me, Your Life Is Waiting* op. cit., p. 212

your attention out of the past and into the present.

Forgiveness not only helps you to become healthier emotionally, it also has a positive impact on your physical health. Medical studies have confirmed that death rates from certain illnesses are higher among people in psychological distress. Holding on to resentment is just such a form of distress, because it puts you into a position where you are inadvertently storing negative energy in the very cells of your body— energy that can ultimately manifest itself as some type of illness.

While forgiveness does have a positive effect on both emotional and physical health, many people still find it very difficult to practice it. Some have this difficulty because they were conditioned to accept the Old Testament "eye-for-an-eye" mentality, others, because they believe that forgiving means condoning whatever inappropriate behavior occurred. The truth is that forgiveness does not mean that what occurred was in any way acceptable, it merely means releasing the negative feelings you have regarding the matter.

Although many believe that practicing forgiveness is nearly impossible in some instances, there is nothing that cannot be forgiven once you come to understand that forgiving is all about letting go of the toxic thoughts and emotions within you.

Though the media tends to almost deify individuals who choose to forgive the perpetrator of a violent act for instance, all of us have the potential to act in the same way. Just as the life force itself forgives you every time you hurt yourself, as an individual aspect of that Divine consciousness you too have within you the same potential to be forgiving.

When you hold on to resentment, the only person you are really hurting is yourself. This is because typically the one who 'hurt' you has already left the matter behind while you remain mired in the past. There is a spiritual solution to this problem, and that is to make it a daily practice to call that person into your consciousness, and extend forgiveness to them until all of your feelings of resentment dissolve. To assist you in this process, a helpful forgiveness prayer was provided in the text of this chapter.

This chapter also pointed out the importance of remembering the words of Jesus as he neared his death: "Forgive them Father, for they know not what they do." While many may feel that people are aware of what they are doing, the reality is that all individuals are simply doing the best they know how to do at any particular time, given the level of their awareness of spiritual principles.

People are usually so focused on their own life that they are, for the most part, unaware of what anyone else is experiencing at the time. For this reason, it is vital that you learn not to take things personally, for other people live in their own dream, in their own mind, and therefore are in a completely different world than the one in which you live.

In addition to forgiving others, it is crucial that you learn to forgive yourself as well. No matter how poorly you may have behaved, whatever you have done in the past is over, and simply put, you would not be the person you are today without that experience. Like everyone else, you were simply doing the best you knew how to do at the time, so release any feelings of self-condemnation. To assist you in this process, a helpful prayer for self-forgiveness was provided in the text of this chapter.

As you proceed in your spiritual growth, you will eventually reach the point where you come to understand a simple but powerful truth about forgiveness—that in order to forgive, you must have first assigned blame. Once you do accept that at some level you do attract (or create) everything that you experience in your life, there is no longer any need to forgive anyone.

Reaching this level of awareness takes time, of course, for some nasty things can happen to you that you certainly would not have consciously chosen. Yet we know from Chapter 4 that the real reason you experience negative 'surprises' in your life is that you are not always conscious of the signals (i.e., thoughts, feelings) you are sending out into the world.

If you are unable to accept this premise, then understand that whenever you blame, you only weaken yourself. Why? Because you put yourself into a position where both your feelings and your state-of-mind are always at the mercy of someone else's behavior.

It is therefore far better to accept complete responsibility for your life, and acknowledge that whatever circumstances you encounter contain within them a valuable lesson that you most definitely need to learn.

Related Reading

Eric Butterworth, *Discover the Power Within You*: Chapter 12

Deepak Chopra, *Ageless Body, Timeless Mind*: Part One

Louise Hay, *You Can Heal Your Life*: Chapter 1

Caroline Myss, *Why People Don't Heal and How They Can*: Chapter 1

Caroline Myss, *Anatomy of the Spirit*: Chapter 4

Dr. Joseph Murphy, *The Power of Your Subconscious Mind*: Chapter 17

Dr. Wayne W. Dyer, *You'll See It When You Believe It*: Chapter 7

Don Miguel Ruiz, *The Four Agreements*: Chapter 3

Lynn Grabhorn, *Excuse Me, Your Life Is Waiting*: Chapter Nine

---

This ends our discussion about spiritual principles. The next and final chapter of *Spirituality Simplified*, which is called "The Path of Spiritual Growth," features an assortment of information designed to help you in your efforts to grow spiritually, including a discussion about a group of self-help techniques that I have found to be very valuable in my own spiritual development.

10: The Path of Spiritual Growth

Let every creature I see,
Be a brother and a friend to me,
Let every step that I take
Leave the footprints of a warrior
Along the spirit trail.[111]

DAN FOGELBERG
"THE SPIRIT TRAIL"

If you have read this far, it is likely that you have a serious interest in moving further along on the path of spiritual growth. From my experience while traveling this course, I can confidently say that once you begin in earnest to seek a deeper understanding of yourself, as well as the nature of existence itself, it's impossible to turn back. The more you open your mind to new ideas and concepts, the more you will want to explore. There is no way around it; it actually gets into your blood.

This discovery is a fascinating process; one that is incredibly rewarding, and at times very demanding as well, simply because spiritual growth requires that you step out of your comfort zone. It also requires that you become increasingly open-minded, and focus more and more of your attention on the present (i.e., on this life), rather than looking toward the potential afterlife rewards typically touted by organized religion.

Traversing this path is a lot like walking a high wire without a safety net, because unlike traditional religious practice there is no rigid dogma that exists to provide you with all of the 'answers'. Instead, on this path *you* take on the responsibility for finding your own answers to questions such as: Who or what is God? What is the proper code of conduct for me to follow? What is the purpose of my life? What is the meaning of life in general?

---

[111] Daniel Fogelberg, Copyright © 1990 by EMI April Music Inc./Hickory Grove Music (ASCAP) (All rights reserved. Used by permission.) From the CD *Wild Places*, (CBS Records and manufactured by Epic Records. 1990).

DEVELOPING "YOUR" SPIRITUAL PHILOSOPHY

Who decides what is true,
And what is not true?
We do, you and I. [112]

TODD RUNDGREN
"I LOVE MY LIFE"

The decision to take responsibility for discovering your inner 'truth' requires that you embark on a quest to develop your own spiritual philosophy. This does not automatically mean you must completely discard your traditional religious beliefs, but it does require that you be willing to *question* literally every aspect of what you have been taught. It also means that you learn to challenge everything you hear and read as you move along this path, including the contents of this book.

In other words, you no longer simply accept something based solely on what another person's religious doctrine, or philosophical author tells you is true. Instead, you closely examine it and ask yourself if that truth actually *feels* right to you. If the insight or concept doesn't resonate positively within you, this is usually a clear signal that it is time for you to put it aside and replace it with something that will.

The following passage from Michael Newton's book *Destiny of Souls* confirms how very important it is for each of us to define our own spiritual truth:

> *Because each of us is a unique being different*
> *from all others, it is incumbent upon those*
> *who desire internal peace to find their own spirituality.*
> *When we totally align ourselves to belief systems*

---

[112] Todd Rundgren, Copyright © 1990 by Fiction Music, Inc. adm. By Warner Tamerlane Pub. Corp (BMI). (All rights reserved. Used by permission.) From the CD *Nearly Human*, (Warner Bros. Records, Inc., a Time Warner Company. 1989).

based upon the experience of other people, I feel we lose
something of our individuality in the process.
The road to self-discovery and shaping a philosophy
not designed by the doctrines of organizations
takes effort but the rewards are great. [113]

Many traditional religionists might argue that having 'faith' means
we may not question established religious doctrine, for the sheer act
of doubting what we have been taught to believe is to be considered
blasphemous behavior. As this quotation from Fr. Anthony
DeMello illustrates, however, that is really not what faith is all about:

An openness to the truth, no matter what the consequences,
no matter where it leads you and when you don't
even know where it's going to lead you. That's faith.
Not belief, but faith. Your beliefs give you a lot of security,
but faith is insecurity. You don't know.
You're ready to follow and you're open,
you're wide open! You're ready to listen. [114]

This doesn't mean that you become gullible and immediately accept
new information to replace the old, but instead you learn to question
everything – new *and* old – with an open mind. It is also essential
for you to understand there is nothing at all irreverent about questioning traditional religious concepts, for even Buddha himself cautioned
against blindly embracing his teachings when he said:

Monks and scholars must not accept my words out of respect,
but must analyze them the way that a goldsmith
analyzes gold, by cutting, scraping, rubbing, melting. [115]

---

[113] Michael Newton, Ph. D., *Destiny of Souls* (St. Paul: Llewellyn Publications, 2002)
p. 398

[114] Anthony DeMello, *Awareness*, op. cit., p. 18

[115] The Bodhisatta, 624-560 BC

In developing your own spiritual philosophy, it is very important that you, too, adopt a similar approach.

Additionally, as mentioned in Chapter 1, you can accelerate your spiritual growth by not limiting yourself with respect to what types of self-development books you will read, tapes you will listen to, or seminars and workshops you will attend. Even if some of the content you encounter appears to be a bit 'out there', you never know what gems you may uncover as you proceed through the remainder of the material.

I know this to be true, since on my own shelves there are a number of books that at first glance contained a lot of material that either didn't interest me, or was in my judgment, somewhat bizarre. Interestingly, it was within many of those same books that I ultimately found incredibly inspirational and/or thought-provoking passages.

In several instances it was necessary to read perhaps a hundred pages to find even one such passage, but in the end the discovery was well worth the reading time invested. I experienced essentially the same thing with various self-help audio programs as well; there was *always* something of value to be found within.

Before leaving this subject, it is important to note there are many who would argue that the development of individualized spiritual philosophies is potentially problematic, particularly given the so-called natural tendency of human beings to be self-serving. In other words, if people are left up to their own devices, what feels spiritually right to them may not be in the best interests of the aggregate society or culture.

In response to this, one need merely look at the success that organized religion as a whole has had in fostering peace and goodwill throughout the world; as discussed in Chapter 8, much of the ongoing conflict in the world is based on some form of religious disagreement. So, could things really become any worse if people assumed the responsibility for developing their own spiritual philosophies? From my perspective, they could only improve.

DEVELOPING A SPIRITUAL PRACTICE

Now you long to be delivered,
From this world of pain and strife,
That's a sorry substitution
For a spiritual life.[116]

DON HENLEY
"THEY'RE NOT HERE, THEY'RE NOT COMING"

In addition to building your own spiritual philosophy, it is equally important for you to develop a spiritual practice as well. To clarify, *practice* in this sense means more than just participation in conventional religious services, it means making spiritual growth work an integral part of your daily routine. When used in this context, *work* refers to the use of prayer, affirmations, meditation, and other techniques for the purpose of elevating your consciousness, and creating different results in your life (e.g., improved relationships, greater abundance, better health, and so on).

Meditation

Since the use of prayer and affirmations was addressed in Chapter 2, I will now focus on meditation, an activity that has traditionally been associated with Eastern spiritual traditions. Like many people in the West, for years I equated meditation with the visual image of monks in saffron robes sitting rigid with their legs crossed in the classic Lotus position.

While this image is reality in some cultures, as this passage from Stuart Wilde attests, effective meditative practice does not require that one assume an uncomfortable physical posture, or behave in some prescribed, ritualistic way:

Meditation need not be complicated.
Some will tell you that nothing less than sitting

---

[116] Don Henley/Stan Lynch, Copyright © 2000 Wisteria Music BMI/WB Music Corp./Matanzas Music (ASCAP) (All rights reserved. Used by permission.) From the CD *Inside Job*, (Warner Bros. Records, Inc., a Time Warner Company. 2000).

cross-legged in the lotus position, ohm'ing yer ohms
in the temple, will do. In fact, any meditation
which is painful or uncomfortable to perform is
distracting in my view. Okay, so you've got your robes on
and you can stick your toe in your ear, big deal. . . .
Excuse me! What's it for? . . . Any ol' meditation style
is just fine; it doesn't have to be a great
performance unless you want it that way.[117]

Although Mr. Wilde does put a humorous spin on the subject of meditation, I believe that his admonitions regarding its practice should be taken very seriously. In my excess of ten years' experience with meditation on an almost daily basis, I have never adhered to any specific disciplines with respect to posture, dress, or methodology. Instead, I have made my best efforts to allocate a certain amount of time each day (usually 24 minutes, or one minute per every hour in the day) to sitting down on a comfortable chair in a quiet room, with my feet firmly planted on the floor, the shades/curtains drawn and the phones turned off.

During these meditation periods, I admit that I am typically unable to completely silence my mind for more than a couple of seconds at a time, but oh, how wonderful it feels to have that momentary connection to the God-Force or the "field of all possibilities" as Deepak Chopra often refers to it. There really is no way that I can adequately describe what these moments are like, except to say that I have never experienced a more peaceful feeling in my life.

In addition to providing me with access to moments of pure tranquility, meditation serves to reduce my heart rate and relax every other part of my body as well. So much so that sometimes when I finish a session, my body feels more rested than it does after an entire night's sleep. It should be noted, however, that such benefits

---

[117] Stuart Wilde, *Infinite Self*, op. cit., p. 100

may not be realized quickly; they manifest over time as you become more proficient at learning to sit still for more than a few minutes at one time. In my case, it took a few years to get to the point where I was able to achieve those few moments of pure silence.

For this reason, it is important that you adopt the perspective that meditation is an activity that you will practice for the rest of your life. This does not mean that you absolutely *must* meditate in the same place for the same amount of time every single day, it requires only that you make it a custom to allocate some time each day to being silent.

For example, on those days when your schedule won't permit you to spend 24 minutes in meditation, perhaps you will be able to put aside just ten minutes for it; maybe only five. The point is that you must make a daily effort to provide yourself with at least some time for quieting your mind and communicating with your Higher Self.

If your knowledge of meditation is limited, the good news is that there are a number of 'how-to' books, audio, and video programs available which focus on this important subject. Visit websites like Amazon.com, BN.com (Barnes & Noble), or stop by your favorite full-service bookstore and you will find a large variety of titles.

I recommend that you take the time to carefully review several alternatives prior to purchasing, and then once your selection is made, stay with that particular approach for at least six months. If by the end of that time you aren't satisfied with the results, go ahead and try something different. In my case, I worked with perhaps five different techniques and ultimately developed my own unique method that draws beneficial bits and pieces from each of them.

As you become more adept in your meditative practice, it will become easier for you to hear the 'quiet voice' of the God-Force (or Spirit), and if your experience is anything like mine, you will learn firsthand that the Biblical adage "Ask and ye shall receive" is quite literal. In that regard, not long after I began practicing meditation, it became a daily routine for me to ask the following question just at the close of my session: *"God-within, what is it that you wish me to know today?"* Provided I am able to truly quiet my mind, I always receive some type of insightful or inspirational thought in response to that question.

Sometimes it is in the form of a song lyric, other times it's a brief excerpt from a book, and still other times it is merely words of encouragement. In all instances, the messages are quite relevant to whatever issues I am experiencing in my life at the time. If you choose to ask this question on a regular basis, and sincerely pay close attention, I believe that over time you, too, will receive a variety of such valuable insights.

In addition to asking that relatively broad question, there are times when I will pose a very specific inquiry, and once again, I always receive the answer I need. The response is not immediate in all cases, but invariably the answer arrives. For example, when I sat down to write one of the early chapters in this book, I lacked direction with respect to the specific topics that needed to be addressed.

One morning, at the close of my meditation period, I asked for guidance on this issue, and after several minutes had received no insights whatsoever. Prior to going to sleep that same night I asked again, and by the following morning there was still no clear inspiration on how to proceed. This stalemate continued for a few more days, until suddenly one morning the proverbial dam broke loose, and in only a few seconds the exact topics that needed to be covered literally rushed into my mind.

This was an amazing experience; one which thoroughly convinced me that we can receive an answer to any question we pose, provided, of course, that we are willing to quiet our minds, and are truly *open* to receiving the guidance we claim to desire. Therefore, if you really want to know what do about something, *ask* for guidance from the higher part of you! For example, if you need advice about your career or a particular relationship, *ask*! If you want guidance regarding a major personal or financial decision, *ask*! The answer *must* come for the simple reason that you are always in contact with that higher intelligence that supports all life.

SELF-HELP TECHNIQUES AND PERSONAL/SPIRITUAL GROWTH

During more than a decade on the path of spiritual and personal growth, I have encountered a large number of so-called self-help techniques, and some of these have become very valuable to me. In the balance of this section, I will provide you with introductory information about five such techniques, and some background regarding my experiences with them.

Fr. Anthony DeMello's "Four Steps to Wisdom"

No resource has had a more profound impact on my spiritual growth than the live recording of a workshop by the late Fr. Anthony DeMello called *Wake Up to Life* (referenced previously in Chapter 7: *Abundance*). After just one session – a mere seven hours – my life was forever changed for the better.

DeMello's *Wake Up to Life* is inspirational and thought provoking, and his presentation style is both entertaining and forthright in nature. Throughout the course of this seminar, he shares many valuable insights on a wide variety of subjects, and provides a very systematic approach to dealing with negative emotions to which he refers as the "Four Steps to Wisdom." Each of these steps is summarized in the following excerpt from *Awareness, The Perils and Opportunities of Reality*: the book version of *Wake Up to Life*:

> *The first thing you need is*
> *awareness of your negative feelings. . . .*
> *Get in touch with those feelings first. . . .*
> *The second step, is to understand that the feeling*
> *is in you, not in reality. . . .*
> *So stop trying to change reality. That's crazy! . . .*
> *The third step: Never identify with that feeling.*

It has nothing to do with the "I."
Don't define your essential self
in terms of that feeling. . . .
The fourth step: Understand that when
you change, everything changes.[118]

The beauty of this approach is that it is practical, simple to understand, and easily put into practice. Based on my experience working with this technique, if you will begin to apply them in your own life, I truly believe that your relationships and overall peace of mind will improve.

For complete information regarding the Four Steps to Wisdom, read pages 78–89 of *Awareness, The Perils and Opportunities of Reality*, by Fr. Anthony DeMello.

Lynn Grabhorn's "Four Steps to Deliberate Creation"

Like DeMello's *Awareness*, the book *Excuse Me, Your Life Is Waiting* by Lynn Grabhorn is also a very entertaining and inspirational work. It is so captivating that once I began reading, it became almost impossible to put the book down.

The basic premise of this book is that how we *feel* about something is even more critical than what we *think* about it. What Ms. Grabhorn promotes is that you need to learn to be very diligent about not making a habit of placing strong emotions behind negative thoughts (e.g., worry, despair) that enter into your mind. More importantly, you must also master the ability to focus your feeling energy on what it is that you *do* want to create in your life.

Within the book, Ms. Grabhorn crystallizes her philosophy into what she calls the "Four Steps to Deliberate Creation," each of which is identified in a clearly defined and easily understood way.

Here are the four steps to deliberate creation,
the four steps that are guaranteed—that's right,

---

[118] Anthony DeMello, *Awareness*, op. cit., p. 79–80; p. 89

guaranteed—to bring into your life whatever is your passion
and much, much more. They are guaranteed because they are
universal law, the basic principles from which all creation
has sprung. Now they are yours if you want them.

Step 1: Identify what you DON'T want.
Step 2: From that, identify what you DO want.
Step 3: Get into the feeling place of what you want.
Step 4: Expect, listen, and allow it to happen.

That's it. That's all there is to it.
As you get into the swing of this remarkable new journey,
things seem to magically change in every area of your life.
Worries, concerns, doubts, and fears go from a constant
ever present little hum to an uncommon occurrence
in a matter of weeks, and you can actually see it
and feel it happening every day.[119]

The sensible nature of this approach is most appealing. Too often, people focus on what they don't want rather than what they do, simply because it is habitual to be more interested in avoiding pain rather than in pursuing pleasure. The tendencies of pain-avoidance are understandable; pain is unpleasant and causes deep fears to surface in many. However, by focusing thoughts and feelings on avoiding pain, we 'flow' our feeling-energy directly toward the things we so sincerely wish to avoid.

To assist you in working with these four steps, the book includes many valuable and easy-to-use exercises. Some are designed to help you learn to promptly catch yourself whenever you are flowing your feeling energy toward a *Don't want*, while others are aimed at teaching you to more easily get yourself into the feeling place of what you *Do* want.

---

[119] Lynn Grabhorn, *Excuse Me, Your Life is Waiting*, op. cit., pp. 22-23.

I have personally put these exercises into practice, and have been
very pleased with the results. For this reason and more, I strongly
advocate this book as a spiritual growth resource.

Don Miguel Ruiz's "The Four Agreements"

Don Miguel Ruiz's *The Four Agreements* is a compelling book that
provides a straightforward, easy-to-understand methodology for
improving one's quality of life. In this engaging work, Ruiz first
reveals the source of self-limiting beliefs that tend to rob people of
joy and create needless suffering. He then recommends a technique
for overcoming these beliefs: adopt four new *agreements* with respect
to how they approach the world and conduct their lives. Each of
these agreements is summarized below:

> *The first agreement is to be impeccable with your word.*
> *It sounds very simple, but it is very, very powerful....*
> *The second agreement is don't take anything personally. . . .*
> *Nothing other people do is because of you.*
> *It is because of themselves. . . .*
> *The third agreement is don't make assumptions.*
> *The problem with making assumptions is that we believe*
> *they are the truth....*
> *The fourth agreement is about the action of the first three:*
> *Always do your best. Under any circumstance,*
> *always do your best, no more and no less.*[120]

The preceding passage is a snippet of Ruiz's work, selected especially to pique your interest in reading the entire book. The simplicity of his approach is particularly appealing, so much so that I have
come to believe that *The Four Agreements* is a 'must' read for anyone
on the path of spiritual growth.

---

[120] Don Miguel Ruiz, *The Four Agreements*, op. cit., p. 25–26; 47–48; 63–64; 75

Wayne Dyer's "Meditations for Manifesting"

Wayne Dyer's *Meditations for Manifesting* are powerful meditative techniques designed to assist you in creating that which you desire to experience in life. There is a morning and evening meditation, each of which relies on the repetition of a specific *sound* (i.e., Aaah and Om respectively). Both are discussed in detail in Chapter 7 of Dyer's book called *Manifest Your Destiny*, and the meditations themselves are available on both cassette tape and CD.

In summary, Dyer proposes that sound can be used to alter our own vibrational frequency so as to consciously attract people, things, and situations into our lives. This excerpt from *Manifest Your Destiny* describes the basic theory behind this concept:

> *Keep in mind that sound is the vibrational frequency*
> *between the world of solid matter or form as we know it*
> *and the higher vibrational frequencies of the formless world*
> *of universal spirit. Learning how to use sound is a way*
> *of harnessing its power for manifesting thought*
> *into the world of form. Manifesting is knowing how to*
> *make contact with that spiritual vibrational frequency*
> *while we are living inside a body in a materialized world.*[121]

While sound meditation may appear at first glance to be a somewhat unconventional approach, recall from Chapter 3 that the spoken word does indeed have enormous creative power, particularly when backed by strong emotions.

My first exposure to this concept left me skeptical at best about the idea that I could create what I desired by sitting and chanting *aaah* and *ohm* for several minutes each day. Skepticism notwithstanding, I put this approach into practice in the late 1990s, intent on focusing on creating a specific amount of weekly income for my technical writing business. In particular, I would begin the practice

---

[121] Wayne W. Dyer, *Manifest Your Destiny*, op. cit., p. 114

anew each Saturday with a revenue goal in mind, and then concentrate on that same amount through the following Friday.

Interestingly, after just a few short weeks, I was actually able to manifest at least what I had established as the income goal for the period, and often much more. In addition, over a period of years, I have continued with this practice and have generally been very pleased with the results. For this reason, I highly recommend their use as part of any spiritual growth practice.

Debbie Ford's "Shadow Process"

The Dark Side of the Light Chasers by Debbie Ford is a fascinating book that draws upon the works of Carl Jung, the renowned Swiss psychologist who coined the term "shadow self." According to Jung, the shadow self is that part in each of us containing all the aspects of ourselves that we fear, and which we have attempted to hide, suppress, or deny. This so-called 'dark side' resides deep within our consciousness, hidden from others and ourselves as well.

Debbie Ford's work is focused on leading people through the process of first acknowledging the existence of their shadow selves, and then learning to see the gifts they offer. As this passage from the book illustrates, Ms. Ford believes that uncovering our shadows is key to transforming our lives:

> *Instead of trying to suppress our shadows,*
> *we need to unconceal, own and embrace the very things*
> *we are most afraid of facing. By "own" I mean acknowledge*
> *that a quality belongs to you. "It is the shadow*
> *that holds the clues," says the spiritual teacher*
> *and author Lazaris. "The shadow holds the*
> *secret of change, change that can affect you on a*
> *cellular level, change that can affect your very DNA."*
> *Our shadows hold the essence of who we are.*
> *They hold our most treasured gifts.*
> *By facing these aspects of ourselves, we become free*

to experience our glorious totality: the good and the bad,
the dark and the light. It is by embracing all of who we are
that we earn the freedom to choose what we do in this world.
As long as we keep hiding, masquerading, and projecting
what is inside us, we have no freedom to be,
and no freedom to choose.[122]

Although shadow work is not a new therapeutic concept, Debbie Ford brings a fresh perspective to it through a unique combination of illuminating personal stories and highly practical exercises. Based on my experience working with many of the exercises found in *The Dark Side of the Light Chasers*, I am convinced that shadow process work can be of immense value to anyone on the path of personal and spiritual growth.

OTHER SPIRITUAL/PERSONAL GROWTH RESOURCES

While books, tapes, and our own practice can usually provide us with what we need as we traverse the path of spiritual and personal growth, there are obviously times in life when outside assistance is required to get us past a particular problem or obstacle. When we encounter such situations, there are resources into which we can tap: most notably conventional psychologists and individuals with clairvoyant skills.

Psychologists and Psychiatrists

Psychologists and psychiatrists can be of great value to us in our healing efforts, particularly when we are dealing with problems related to conditioning received early in life. From personal experience, psychological therapy was very helpful in my overcoming some deeply held beliefs that had, for many years, prevented me from having a successful, long-term love relationship.

I prefer the Rational Emotive Therapy (RET) approach which was

---

[122] Debbie Ford, *The Dark Side of the Light Chasers*, op. cit., p. 2

discussed in Chapter 7, simply because its use of a scientific method resonates with my analytical nature.

There are, of course, numerous other therapeutic approaches available, so it is prudent to do thorough investigation in this area (i.e., on the Web or in a library) to help you select the one that feels right for you. From there, you will need to identify the appropriate practitioner, and this is essentially a matter of learning as much as you can about prospective therapists prior to making a choice. Referrals from trusted sources will be especially valuable to you when conducting a search of this nature.

Once you have selected a therapist and initiated the treatment process, be certain to pay close attention to how you are *connecting* with that person. If you experience any feelings of uneasiness that persist for more than a session or two, don't hesitate to terminate that association and begin a search for a suitable alternative.

Clairvoyants and Psychics

While conventional psychology can help heal a variety of life issues, it is by no means a cure-all; there clearly are times when we need assistance that is more spiritually based. Fortunately, gifted individuals exist who have the ability to provide us with insights into ourselves that psychologists simply cannot. The people of whom I speak are those that have legitimate clairvoyant skills, including psychics and those that possess the ability to communicate with spiritual entities outside the earth plane (i.e., spirit channels).

If you are doubtful that such people truly exist I would not be surprised, for as mentioned in Chapter 1 at one point in the past I felt the exact same way. However, during the past ten years I've had the pleasure of meeting and interacting with a few of these individuals, and can confidently say that each one of them does, indeed, possess amazing psychic capabilities.

In particular, these people were not only capable of providing me with valuable insights into my potential future (*potential* because we all have freewill choice to alter our current path), but they also had the ability to look into the past and help me uncover key events that continued to affect my present life in a negative way. This type of assistance has proven to be invaluable over the years, and for this reason I strongly advocate working with these types of individuals on an *occasional* basis, as one traverses the path of spiritual growth.

Identifying Competent Clairvoyant Resources

There are probably hundreds, if not thousands, of competent clairvoyants and spirit channels within the United States; no doubt many more practice throughout the rest of the world as well. The challenge is how to locate the person that's right for you.

As mentioned in Chapter 3, the most effective way to identify a truly gifted clairvoyant is to ask for a referral from someone else who is on a path of personal discovery. In this regard, I suggest that you do some networking among your like-minded friends, and build a list of potential sources of clairvoyant services. Additionally, to assist you in this area, the *Links* page of my web-site (www.spiritsimple.com) includes a list of clairvoyant individuals with whom I have personally worked and been very satisfied[‡].

AVOIDING SPIRITUAL PRIDE

As you proceed along the path of spiritual growth, it can at times be very tempting to feel that your own philosophy is superior to that of others, particularly those who continue to strictly adhere to traditional religious principles.

When such feelings arise, it is very important to:

1. Remind yourself they are not coming from your Higher Self, but are instead originating from your ego-self, and

2. Promptly dismiss them from your consciousness.

[‡] The clairvoyant individuals referenced on www.spiritsimple.com are presented as a guide in assisting you when embarking on your own path of discovery; no assurances or guarantees are made or implied. As with your own individuality, each session and the ensuing results will be unique to you.

Feelings of spiritual pride are very dangerous because they only serve to reinforce the feeling of separateness between yourself and others. As we learned in Chapter 6: *Oneness*, whenever you judge another you are seeing that person as *you* are rather than how *they* are. Therefore, always make your best effort to remember that *your* way is not *the* way, and as such, you have no right to feel spiritually superior to anyone. Additionally, remind yourself that what they have chosen to accept as their inner 'truth' is exactly what they need at this point in their spiritual evolution.

Finally, whenever you do feel the temptation to judge those following a conventional religious path, try to remember the guidance offered in this insightful passage:

> *You must have love and understanding for those who seek*
> *their salvation in a structured way—a way they understand—*
> *for they choose to have set rules. These souls often seek*
> *direction from others not recognizing the power and*
> *Love within their own souls.*
> *They have come to see their religion as being able to place*
> *their faith in what they do not understand.*
> *Such souls feel they must have*
> *something stronger than themselves.*[123]

SPIRITUAL GROWTH IS A JOURNEY NOT A DESTINATION

To bring both this chapter and book to a close, I want to emphasize that the purpose of pursuing the path of spiritual growth is not to reach a specific destination, but to enjoy the entire journey of evolving and coming to a greater and greater awareness of *who you really are*. Each day brings you new opportunities to heal yourself physically, mentally, and emotionally, and also to discover more about your true nature, as well as that of the entire Universe. Additionally,

---

[123] Diandra, *A New Day is Dawning*, op. cit., p. 175

each discovery you make helps to raise your consciousness and bring you even closer to the God-Force that created you.

SUMMING IT ALL UP

Once you embark upon the path of spiritual growth, it truly becomes impossible to turn back. The more you open yourself up to new ideas and concepts, the more you will be inspired to continue to explore. It is a process that is both rewarding and challenging, for it definitely requires that you step outside of where you feel comfortable. Growing spiritually also demands that you become increasingly open-minded, and that you learn to focus your attention more on the 'here and now' rather than on seeking rewards in some afterlife.

Unlike conventional religious practice, the path of spiritual growth is more precarious because there is no rigid doctrine to provide you with all of the answers. On this path, it is you, and you alone, who assume the responsibility for finding them. To discover your inner truth effectively requires that you develop your own spiritual philosophy, meaning you no longer simply accept established religious truths as absolute, but instead carefully evaluate them to determine if they actually *feel* right to you.

To further hasten your spiritual growth, don't limit yourself with respect to the type of books, tapes, and seminars you're willing to experience. Even though some of the content may appear to be a bit bizarre, you can never tell when or where you'll come across truly life-changing information.

In addition to creating a personal spiritual philosophy, it is just as important for you to create your own spiritual practice. When used in this context, practice means more than just being involved in traditional religious practices, it means making spiritual growth work part of your daily routine.

With respect to the practice of meditation, there is no need for you to follow rigid principles regarding methodology or attire, as this tends to draw your attention away from the primary reasons for doing it: relaxing your body, silencing your mind, and tapping into the energy of the God-Force. Meditation need not be complicated; all you really need to do is discipline yourself to allocate some time each day to sit down on a comfortable chair in quiet room.

As you continue doing this, bit-by-bit you will find yourself able to experience moments of complete mental stillness that are accompanied by a feeling of unparalleled peace. In addition, you will notice that physical benefits will gradually manifest as well (e.g., lower resting heart rate). None of this will happen overnight of course, and for that reason it is necessary that you accept that meditation is something you need to practice for your entire lifetime.

Whatever meditation method you employ, you will find that, over time, it will become increasingly easy for you to receive important insights from the God-Force (or Spirit) during your meditations. If you ask a question, you will indeed receive some type of response because you truly are always in contact with your Creator.

This chapter also included brief summaries of five valuable self-help techniques, as well as my experiences working with them. They are: Fr. Anthony DeMello's *Four Steps to Wisdom*, Lynn Grabhorn's *Four Steps to Deliberate Creation*, Don Miguel Ruiz's *The Four Agreements*, Wayne Dyer's *Meditations for Manifesting*, and Debbie Ford's *Shadow Process*. All of these techniques can be of great assistance to anyone on the path of spiritual growth, and for that reason, I encourage you to learn more about each of them.

In addition to books, tapes, and your own daily spiritual practice, there are times when you may need assistance from a third party to get beyond a given obstacle. In such instances, there are other resources you can access, most notably conventional psychologists and individuals with demonstrated clairvoyant skills.

This chapter also talked about the importance of avoiding 'spiritual pride.' When you fall prey to such feelings, you are effectively fostering separation between yourself and your fellow human beings, forgetting that *your* way is not *the* way for everyone else. Be kind and tolerant, continually reminding yourself that every person is just where he or she needs to be at that particular point in their spiritual evolution.

Finally, always remember that the real purpose of following the path of spiritual growth is not to reach a specific destination, but instead it's about enjoying the entire journey and coming to a better and clearer awareness of your true identity.

Related Reading

Michael Newton, Ph.D., *Destiny of Souls*: Chapter 10

Anthony DeMello, *Awareness*: Listen and Unlearn; Four Steps to Wisdom

Stuart Wilde, *Infinite Self*: Step 10

Lynn Grabhorn, *Excuse Me, Your Life Is Waiting*: Chapter One

Don Miguel Ruiz, *The Four Agreements* (in its entirety)

Wayne W. Dyer, *Manifest Your Destiny*: The Seventh Principle

Debbie Ford, *The Dark Side of the Light Chasers*: Chapter 1

Diandra, *A New Day Is Dawning*: Chapter 19

My sincere best wishes to you for a long, inspiring and joyful journey along your own path of spiritual growth.

Epilogue

As I reflect upon the time nearly five years ago when I was first inspired to write *Spirituality Simplified*, I can truthfully say that the idea of actually *publishing* a book someday didn't even cross my mind. My initial intent was to piece together what I had gleaned on my path of self-discovery from the vast amount of materials I had read, as a means of more clearly defining my own life's philosophy. As the years passed and the work progressed, however, I began to feel more and more that this work could be of value to many people in the world.

In fact, by the time I had completed the first six chapters, there developed within me what can only be described as an inner *knowing*, not a belief, (see Chapter 2) that this book was destined to be published. This 'knowing' was not rooted in ego-based awareness, but instead was like a warm, confident feeling within my consciousness that was always with me through all of the obstacles that ultimately arose over the course of the project. Indeed, it was this 'knowing' that enabled me to successfully deal with the challenges that always seem to be associated with such creative endeavors—and believe me, there were a number of them. This project truly was like the proverbial "roller-coaster ride." Times of great progress and excitement were often followed by lengthy delays and disappointment.

What I find most interesting is that throughout the course of this writing and publishing effort, I was regularly presented with opportunities to actually put into practice each of the spiritual principles discussed in the book. This really didn't surprise me, as I read somewhere once that "we teach that which we need to learn"—I just never anticipated that the curriculum would be so difficult at times! And yet, now that *Spirituality Simplified* is in print I can see the perfection in the process. The reality is the only way for me to earn the right to instruct others regarding the application of these principles, was to be able to consistently apply them myself, particularly while in the midst of a project that was so near and dear to my heart, and which required a significant investment in both time and effort.

This is *not* to suggest that things won't tend to *flow* more easily to you when you do make the decision to, in the words of Joseph Campbell, "follow your bliss." The Universe will indeed conspire to support your efforts, but it will do so by bringing to you *all* of the people and situations you need to ensure that you obtain the maximum spiritual benefit from the experience. This essentially means that you must be willing to accept the hardships along with the successes, and arrive at the understanding that there is spiritual value inherent within all of them. Additionally, you need to come to the realization that while the Universe will do *its* part to assist you, the manifestation of your heart's desires also requires *you* to remain doggedly persistent in your efforts.

Appendix

RECOMMENDED READING

Within this book are inspirational and/or thought-provoking passages from nearly forty books related to personal and/or spiritual growth. Having personally read each of these books, I feel that each and every one of them is worth reading, or they would never have been used to provide source material for *Spirituality Simplified*.

With that said, I am also well aware that in today's fast-paced world most people simply do not have the time to read large numbers of books. Therefore, in the table below I have identified ten books that I believe are '*must reads*' for any person seriously interested in the path of personal and spiritual growth. The second table includes a number of other books that I consider to be very worthwhile reading as well.

"Must Read" Books	
Title	*Author*
Dare to Be Yourself	*Alan Cohen*
The Seven Spiritual Laws of Success	*Deepak Chopra*
Awareness, The Perils and Opportunities of Reality	*Fr. Anthony De Mello*
You'll See It When You Believe It	*Dr. Wayne W. Dyer*
Excuse Me, Your Life Is Waiting	*Lynn Grabhorn*
Way of the Peaceful Warrior	*Dan Millman*
The Celestine Prophecy	*James Redfield*
The Four Agreements	*Don Miguel Ruiz*
The Power of Now	*Eckhart Tolle*
Conversations with God, Book 1	*Neale Donald Walsch*
Friendship with God	*Neale Donald Walsch*
Infinite Self	*Stuart Wilde*

"Recommended" Books

Title	Author
Animal Speak	*Ted Andrews*
Creating Affluence	*Deepak Chopra*
Ageless Body, Timeless Mind	*Deepak Chopra*
The Dragon Doesn't Live Here Anymore	*Alan Cohen*
Why Your Life Sucks....and What You Can Do About It	*Alan Cohen*
The Way to Love	*Anthony De Mello*
Manifest Your Destiny	*Wayne W. Dyer*
Real Magic	*Dr. Wayne W. Dyer*
Your Sacred Self	*Dr. Wayne W. Dyer*
There's A Spiritual Solution to Every Problem	*Wayne W. Dyer*
The Dark Side of the Light Chasers	*Debbie Ford*
You Can Heal Your Life	*Louise Hay*
The Quest, A Journey of Spiritual Rediscovery	*Richard and Mary-Alice Jafolla*
Queen of the Sun	*E.J. Michael*
The Laws of Spirit	*Dan Millman*
Living on Purpose	*Dan Millman*
Mutant Message Down Under	*Marlo Morgan*
Reflections on the Art of Living, A Joseph Campbell Companion	*Diane K. Osbon*
Why People Don't Heal and How They Can	*Caroline Myss*
You Can Have It All	*Arnold Patent*
Barefoot Doctor's Guide to the TAO	*Stephen Russell*
You Are The Answer	*Michael J. Tamura*
Born Again, and Again	*John Van Auken*
The New Revelations	*Neale Donald Walsch*
Abundance and Right Livelihood	*Neale Donald Walsch*
Communion with God	*Neale Donald Walsch*
Moments of Grace	*Neale Donald Walsch*

"Recommended" Books (continued)

Title	Author
Affirmations	*Stuart Wilde*
Life Wasn't Meant to Be a Struggle	*Stuart Wilde*
Silent Power	*Stuart Wilde*
The Little Money Bible	*Stuart Wilde*
Whispering Winds of Change	*Stuart Wilde*
A Return to Love	*Marianne Williamson*
God! This Is A Good Book	*Rich Work*
The Seat of the Soul	*Gary Zukav*

Author Contact

If you would care to comment or have questions regarding this book, or if you would like information regarding Jeff's *Spirituality Simplified* workshop and how to arrange for it, please direct your correspondence to:

Jeff Maziarek

E-mail: jam@Spiritsimple.com

Selected Bibliography

I list here many of the writings that have been of immeasurable help in the writing of this book. This bibliography is by no means a complete record of all the works and sources available on this subject, nor is it complete in the list of sources with which I have consulted. This listing indicates the substance and range of reading upon which I have formed my ideas, and I intend it to serve as a convenient beginning reading list for those wishing to pursue the study of spirituality.

Andrews, Ted. *Animal Speak.* St. Paul, MN: Llewellyn Publications, 1999.

Butterworth, Eric. *Discover the Power Within You*, New York, NY: HarperColllins Publishers, 1968.

Chopra, Deepak. *Ageless Body, Timeless Mind.* New York: Harmony Books, 1993.

Chopra, Deepak. *Creating Affluence.* San Rafael, California: New World Library, 1993.

Chopra, Deepak. *The Seven Spiritual Laws of Success.* San Rafael, CA: Amber-Allen Publishing & New World Library, 1994.

Chopra, Deepak. *How To Know God.* New York, NY: Harmony Books, 2000.

Cohen, Alan. *The Dragon Doesn't Live Here Anymore.* New York, NY: A Fawcett Columbine Book, published by Ballantine Books, 1981/1990.

Cohen, Alan. *Dare to be Yourself.* New York, NY: A Fawcett Columbine Book, published by Ballantine Books, 1991.

DeMello, Anthony. *Awareness.* New York, NY: Image Books/ Doubleday, 1992.

Diandra, *A New Day is Dawning.* Naperville, IL: Inward Journey Publishing, 1997.

Dyer, Wayne W. *Manifest Your Destiny*. New York: HarperCollins, 1997.

Dyer, Dr. Wayne W. *You'll See It When You Believe It*. New York, NY: William Morrow and Company, 1989.

Ellis, Dr. Albert. *How to Stubbornly Refuse to Make Yourself Miserable About Anything*. New York, NY: Carol Publishing Group, 1988.

Ford, Debbie. *The Dark Side of the Light Chasers*. New York, NY: Avon Books, 1998.

Foundation for Inner Peace. *A Course in Miracles*. New York, London: Penguin Books, 1975.

Fox, Emmet. *Your Heart's Desire*. Marina del Rey, CA: DeVorss & Co., 1933.

Grabhorn, Lynn. *Excuse Me, Your Life Is Waiting*. Charlottesville, VA: Hampton Roads Publishing Company, Inc., 2000.

Hay, Louise. *You Can Heal Your Life*. Carson, CA: Hay House, Inc., 1984.

Jafolla, Richard and Mary-Alice. *The Quest, A Journey of Spiritual Rediscovery*. Unity Village, MO: Unity Books, 1993.

Michael, E.J., *Queen of the Sun*. New York, NY: HarperCollins Publishers Inc., 1995.

Millman, Dan. *The Laws of Spirit*. Tiburon, CA: H.J. Kramer, Inc., 1995.

Murphy, Dr. Joseph . *The Power of Your Subconscious Mind*. Englewood Cliffs, NJ: Prentice-Hall, Inc., 1963.

Murphy, Dr. Joseph. *The Amazing Laws of Cosmic Mind Power*. W. Nyack, NY: Parker Publishing Company, Inc., 1965.

Myss, Caroline, Ph. D., *Anatomy of the Spirit*. New York, NY: Harmony Books, 1996.

Myss, Caroline, Ph. D., *Why People Don't Heal and How They Can*. New York, NY: Harmony Books, 1997.

Newton, Michael, Ph.D., *Destiny of Souls*. St. Paul, MN: Llewellyn Publications, 2002.

Patent, Arnold M. *You Can Have It All*. Piermont, NY: Money Mastery Publishing, 1984.

Roman, Sanaya. *Spiritual Growth, Being Your Higher Self.* Tiburon, CA: H J Kramer Inc., 1989.

Ruiz, Don Miguel. *The Four Agreements*. San Rafael, CA: Amber-Allen Publishing, 1997.

Tolle, Eckhart. *The Power of Now*. Novato, CA: New World Library, 1999.

Van Auken, John. *Born Again & Again*. Virginia Beach, VA: Inner Vision Publishing Company, 1989.

Walsch, Neale Donald. *Conversations with God, Book 1*. New York, NY: G.P. Putnam's Sons, 1996.

Walsch, Neale Donald. *Conversations with God, Book 2*. Charlottesville, VA: Hampton Roads Publishing Company, Inc., 1997.

Walsch, Neale Donald. *Conversations with God, Book 3*. Charlottesville, VA: Hampton Roads Publishing Company, Inc., 1998.

Walsch, Neale Donald. *Friendship with God*. New York, NY: G.P. Putnam's Sons, 1998.

Wilde, Stuart. *The Quickening*. Carlsbad, CA: Hay House, Inc., 1996.

Wilde, Stuart, *Infinite Self.* Carlsbad, California: Hay House, Inc., 1996.

Wilde, Stuart. *The Little Money Bible*. Carlsbad, California: Hay House, Inc., 1998.

Work, Rich, w/Ann Marie Groth, *Awaken to the Healer Within*. Mosinee, WI: Asini Publishing, 1995.

Yogananda, Paramahansa. *The Law of Success*. Los Angeles, CA: Self Realization Fellowship, 1944.

Selected Discography

Spirituality Simplified includes several quotations from the lyrics* of various pop music songs that directly relate to the particular subject being addressed. The following list summarizes the source material used by the author (* *All passages were used by permission.*)

Ambrosia, *Art Beware*. From the album "Life Beyond L.A". (Warner Bros. Records, Inc. 1978).

The Beatles, *I Am The Walrus*. From the album "Magical Mystery Tour." (The Gramophone Co. Ltd., Northern Songs Ltd. 1967).

Jackson Browne, *The Fuse*. From the album "The Pretender." (Elektra/Asylum Records, a division of Warner Communications, Inc. (now a Time Warner Company) 1976).

Joe Cocker, *Up Where We Belong*. From the CD "The Essential Joe Cocker." (Island Records. 1982), (Karussel International, 1995).

Dan Fogelberg, *Wild Places*. From the CD "Wild Places." (CBS Records and manufactured by Epic Records. 1990).

Dan Fogelberg, *Man in the Mirror*. From the album "Captured Angel." (CBS Records and manufactured by Epic Records/CBS Inc. 1975).

Dan Fogelberg, *Wild Places*. From the CD "Wild Places." (CBS Records and manufactured by Epic Records. 1990).

Don Henley, *Little Tin God*. From the CD "The End of the Innocence." (The David Geffen Company, manufactured exclusively by Warner Bros. Records, Inc., a Time Warner Company. 1988).

Don Henley, *Gimme What You've Got*. From the CD "The End of the Innocence." (The David Geffen Company, manufactured exclusively by Warner Bros. Records, Inc., a Time Warner Company. 1988).

Don Henley, *The Heart of the Matter*. From the CD "The End of the Innocence." (The David Geffen Company, manufactured exclusively by Warner Bros. Records, Inc., a Time Warner Company. 1988).

Don Henley, *My Thanksgiving*. From the CD "Inside Job." (Warner Bros. Records, Inc., a Time Warner Company. 2000).

Don Henley, *They're Not Here, They're Not Coming*. From the CD "Inside Job." (Warner Bros. Records, Inc., a Time Warner Company. 2000).

Todd Rundgren, *No World Order 1.1*. From the CD " No World Order." (Alchemedia Productions. Manufactured and distributed by Forward, a label of Rhino Records, Inc. 1993).

Todd Rundgren, *Proactivity*. From the CD "No World Order." (Alchemedia Productions. Manufactured and distributed by Forward, a label of Rhino Records, Inc. 1993).

Todd Rundgren, *Who's Sorry Now?* From the CD "Second Wind." (Warner Bros. Records, Inc., a Time Warner Company. 1990).

Todd Rundgren, *I Love My Life*. From the CD "Nearly Human." (Warner Bros. Records, Inc., a Time Warner Company. 1989).

Styx, *The Grand Illusion*. From the album "The Grand Illusion." (A&M Records, Inc. 1977).

Triumph, *Fight the Good Fight*. From the album "Allied Forces." (TRC Records. 1981).

Index